HAPPY NEW YEA
PARENT
1
WinterCLASSIC
BRIDGESTONE

Library of Congress Cataloging-in-Publication Data

Parent, Bernie, 1945–
 Unmasked : Bernie Parent and the Broad street bullies / Bernie Parent with Stan Hochman.
 p. cm.
 ISBN 978-1-60078-761-4
 1. Parent, Bernie, 1945– 2. Hockey players—United States—Biography. 3. Philadelphia Flyers (Hockey team) I. Hochman, Stan.
II. Title.
 GV848.5.P28A34 2012
 796.962092—dc23
 [B]

2012018262

This book is available in quantity at special discounts for your group or organization. For further information, contact:

Triumph Books LLC
814 North Franklin
Chicago, Illinois 60610
(312) 337-0747
www.triumphbooks.com

Printed in U.S.A.
ISBN: 978-1-60078-761-4
Design by Patricia Frey

Photos credits: p. xii, xviii, 84, 87, 98, 106, 150, 154, 158, 162, 187, and 189 courtesy of AP Images; p. 20, 22, 23, 25, 27, 28, 31, 33, and 51 courtesy of Bernie Parent; p. 8 and 96 courtesy of Sam Psoras/*Philadelphia Daily News*; p. 13 and 42 courtesy of Lou Zacharias/*Philadelphia Daily News*; p. 46, 52, 92, and 144 courtesy of Elwood P. Smith/*Philadelphia Daily News*; p. 73 courtesy of Will Everly III/*Philadelphia Daily News*; p. 91 courtesy of Daily News Archive/*Philadelphia Daily News*; p. ii, v, vi, vii, viii, x, xiv, xvi, 83, 111, 112, 116, 120, 125, 170, 175, 176, 179, 180, 183, 190, and 198 courtesy of Getty Images; p. 111 courtesy of Al Deans/*Philadelphia Inquirer*; p. 38 and 133 courtesy of Alexander McCaughey/*Philadelphia Inquirer*; p. 64 courtesy of Gerard C. Benene/*Philadelphia Inquirer*; p. 68, 137, and 138 courtesy of Gervase J. Rozanski/*Philadelphia Inquirer*; p. 2, 6, 45, 88, 94, 129, and 130 courtesy of Inquirer Archive/*Philadelphia Inquirer*; p. 5 courtesy of Joseph Conley/*Philadelphia Inquirer*; p. 61, 102, and 141 courtesy of Michael Viola/*Philadelphia Inquirer*; p. 58 and 76 courtesy of Richard M. Titley/*Philadelphia Inquirer*; p. 126 courtesy of Vicki Valerio/*Philadelphia Inquirer*

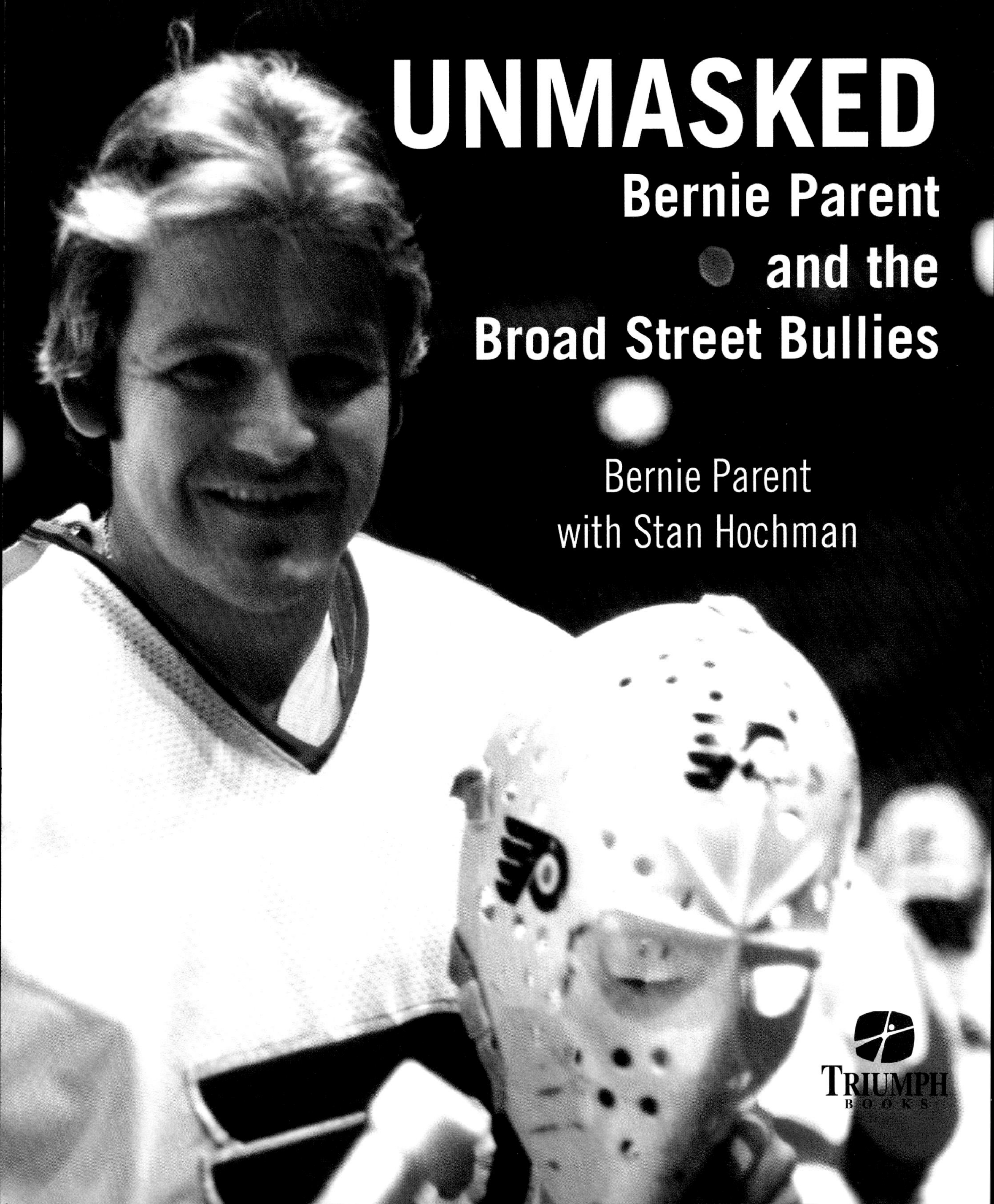

UNMASKED

Bernie Parent and the Broad Street Bullies

Bernie Parent
with Stan Hochman

TRIUMPH
BOOKS

2
PARE

PARENT

BAUER

BERNIE
PARENT

TECH

HOME OF THE
Phillies
Citizens Bank Park
BAUER

FOREWORD

The Broad Street Bullies could never have happened without Bernie Parent in goal. Bernie was the great goaltender we had to have to establish our identity as a team.

Let's face it, some of the penalties we took were borderline ridiculous. Guys like Dave Schultz and Moose Dupont were just hammering people. We led the league in penalty minutes both years we won the Stanley Cup, and every guy on the roster could have been replaced except for one, and that was Bernie.

People wondered if we would welcome Bernie back to our locker room after he bolted from the Philadelphia Blazers during the World Hockey Association playoffs. There was no problem. We looked around and we knew we had a pretty good team. And now, we were adding a great goalie.

We intimidated some teams, sure. But we also had to beat the really good teams, the solid teams. And that's where Bernie did his thing.

He was a fierce competitor. He hated to be scored on. I saw him throw his stick at guys who scored on him in practice.

It's amazing, isn't it? In retirement he looks and sounds like your favorite uncle—kind, gentle, funny. Totally different from the guy who was so intense in practice and in games.

16

He was the greatest goalie in the world for those years, and he felt the pressure of being the greatest goalie in the world. It's probably a good thing he retired when he did, even though he was forced into retirement when that stick came up and jabbed him in the eye.

If he hadn't retired, the pressure might have gotten to him eventually. I know he came to me, when I was managing the team and he could see the toll it was taking, and he said I ought to stop. He told me to stop and smell the roses.

He had 12 shutouts that first year we won the Cup, and 12 more the next year. Our coach, Fred Shero, didn't make a big deal about that. And he didn't think much about the Vezina Trophy, which went to the goalie on the team with the lowest goals-against average.

Freddie didn't want guys playing conservatively to protect the goalie's numbers. He wanted us to play

"He was the greatest goalie in the world for those years, and he felt the pressure of being the greatest goalie in the world."

aggressively. That first year, Bernie was right near the top of the Vezina standings.

That's when Freddie used Bob Taylor in a game against Pittsburgh. Bernie had played in about 44 straight games, and Freddie said it was the Chief's turn.

Taylor gave up something like six goals, but it turned out okay because Bernie wound up tied for the Vezina. I think Freddie was just trying to take some pressure off Bernie.

Freddie was really close to Bernie, and probably understood him better than anyone. They'd even go out together, get half-looped, and drive home together. One night, Bernie decided to have some fun with Freddie, and he told him how to get home after he dropped Bernie off.

Freddie drove around for an hour and a half before he finally got home. The next day at practice, Freddie told the team about it. Then he turned to Bernie and he said, "If you had been navigating for Christopher Columbus, he'd still be out there, trying to discover America."

Bernie handled the pressure with humor, his brand of half-crazy humor. He loved The Three Stooges. And he loved to be outdoors, to hunt. Sometimes he'd go hunting before he came to practice. And he loves that boat of his. I went out with him twice, and got seasick both times. Bernie just loved being out there, driving the boat, enjoying the view. He didn't care if he fished or not.

He'd sit up there, saying, "Isn't this great?" and I was sick and hating the whole thing.

After games, the writers would surround him and he'd say, "Some fun, eh?" That was just his way of handling the pressure.

I remember we were leading Boston 1–0 with nine minutes left in the Stanley Cup Finals.

Faceoff in our end. Bernie waved winger Simon Nolet over and started jabbering at him.

I saw Nolet nearly jump out of his skates. Then he waved at Bernie in disgust. Simon came back to the bench and I asked him, "What did that crazy joker say?"

Simon shrugged and said, "Bernie said he had gotten this brand-new set of golf clubs, so how about we just wrap this thing up so he could go out and use them?"

That was just Bernie's way of dealing with the pressure. And it worked for him.

When it was over and we'd beaten Boston and won the Cup, they handed it to me. I skated over to Bernie. I always called him Bennie, and I said, "Bennie, grab hold of this thing and let's skate it around the rink together."

We couldn't do it, because the ice was jammed with fans and photographers and security guys. But it just seemed right. I certainly hadn't done enough to skate the Cup around by myself.

And we couldn't have won the Stanley Cup without Bernie in goal.

—Bobby Clarke

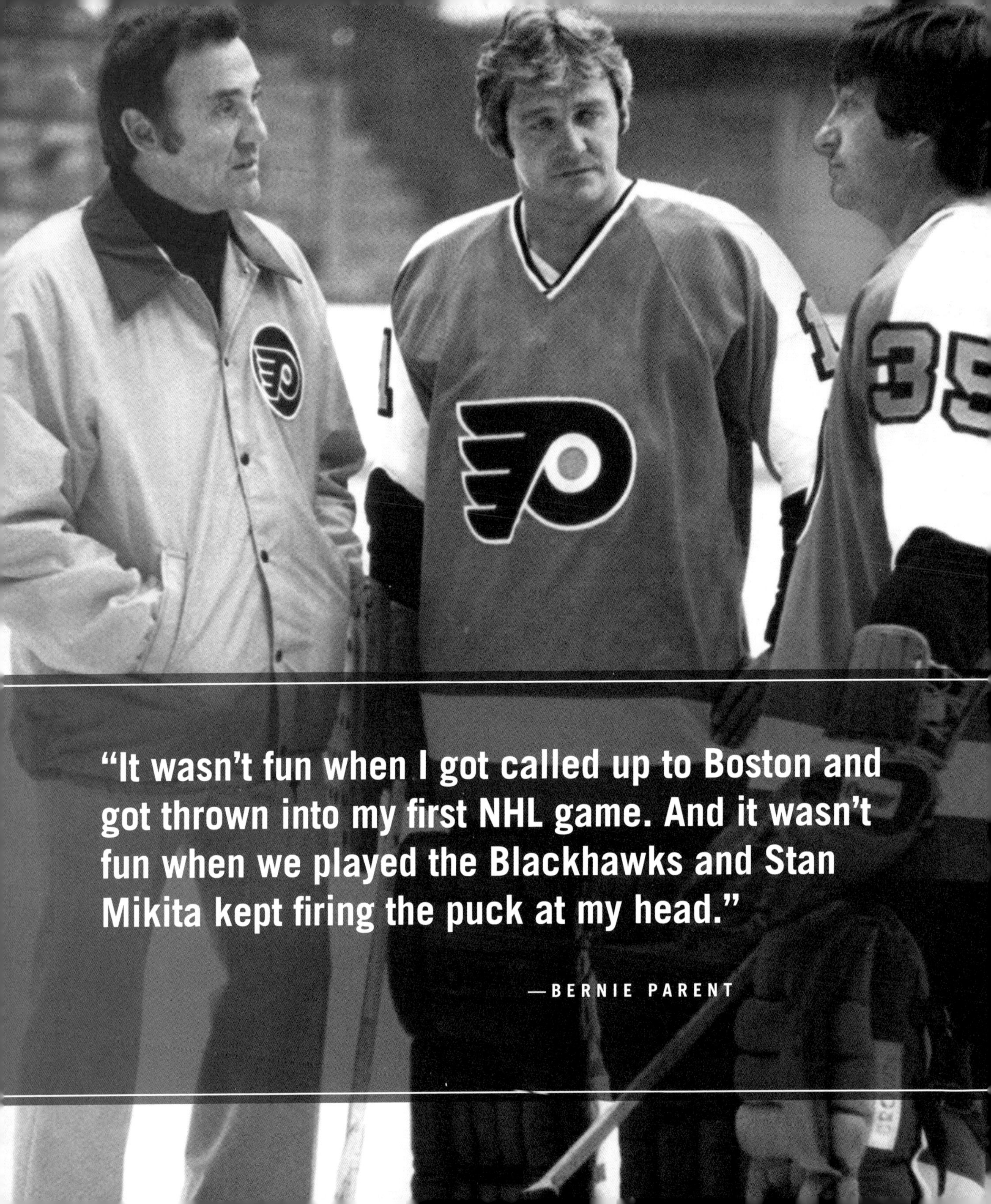

"It wasn't fun when I got called up to Boston and got thrown into my first NHL game. And it wasn't fun when we played the Blackhawks and Stan Mikita kept firing the puck at my head."

—BERNIE PARENT

SOME FUN, EH?

The last time I pulled on the orange-and-black sweater to tend goal for the Philadelphia Flyers was February 17, 1979. That's the day my career ended after a stick blade poked through my mask and into my right eye.

What is that, 30-something years ago?

Yet even today, total strangers come up to me, shake my hand, smile, and say, "Some fun, eh?" I can't blame them. There were nights where I'd face 35 shots and stop 34 of them, nights when we played a man short five or six times because we led the league in penalty minutes, nights when I could still feel the bruise from a blistering Bobby Hull wrist shot I stopped with my right shoulder.

I would come into the locker room, yank off the pads, wipe the sweat off my face, and here came the writers. I'd look up, smile, and say, "Some fun, eh?"

People thought I was some happy-go-lucky guy, acting like I'd just gotten back from a picnic in the park, chuckling my way through the National Hockey League.

In fact, it wasn't even my line. Some advertising agency guy thought it up and had me say it at the end of one of the worst commercials in the history of television.

It all began with that Industrial Valley Bank giveaway in 1975. A lot of Flyers fans already had bumper stickers on their cars that said, "Only the Lord saves more than Bernie Parent."

So the bank organized a Bernie Parent's Savers Club. Savers Club, get it? The deal was, open a savings account for at least $50, and they'd give you an orange windbreaker with my name on it.

They decided to have me do a commercial to promote the thing. It was brutal. How bad was it? My dog, a German shepherd named Tinker Bell, watched it, and when I came home that night, she bit me.

Some people with long memories and a mean streak entertain their friends by trying to sound the way I did in that commercial. "Put your moan-knee in dat bank," they say, "and dey will geeve you a jack-KET with my name on eet."

A sportswriter told me it was so bad, it was good. I thought it was a compliment until I really thought about it. Maybe it was so bad because I still didn't feel comfortable speaking English. Maybe it was so bad because the red light on the camera went on when it was my turn to speak. What goalie in his right mind feels comfortable when a red light goes on?

So I struggled through it. At the end I looked into the camera, smiled, and said, "Some fun, eh?"

It was like magic. That's what people remember, the same way they remember the little old lady who said, "Where's the beef?" in that Wendy's commercial. Somewhere, buried deep in a vault at an IVB bank, there's a copy of that commercial. I hope they never find it.

Hey, it worked. More than 20,000 people opened savings accounts with IVB, many of them for more than $50. So many people signed up in those first few days that they ran out of orange windbreakers and had to ask people to please be patient.

Hockey was never fun.

Okay, maybe when we were kids and played on a frozen pond or on the streets on the outskirts of Montreal. It stayed cold long enough that the ice didn't melt, and they didn't believe in scattering chemicals or salt on it.

Maybe it was fun then, even though I didn't have skates. I played in boots or galoshes. I wore jeans. No referee, no scoreboard, just a bunch of kids in hand-me-down equipment skating up and down the ice and me flopping on my backside, no balance, no idea of what playing the angles meant, just trying to stop the tennis ball or the puck from going in the net.

After that, it was never fun.

It was no fun trying out for the Canadiens junior team. I stuck around for four days before they sent me home. They said I didn't have what it took.

It was no fun signing with Boston, and going off on a train to Niagara Falls, barely speaking English, my equipment stuck with the Rosemont team for weeks. I couldn't practice, couldn't play, and couldn't tell anyone how I really felt.

BERNIE PAREN
SAVERS CLU
LA

JOIN AT
IVB
Industrial Valley Bank
and Trust Company

1
PARENT B.

It wasn't fun when I got called up to Boston and got thrown into my first NHL game. And it wasn't fun when we played the Blackhawks and Stan Mikita kept firing the puck at my head.

I finally told him I'd had enough, and he said he'd decide when enough was enough. So he did it again, and the next time he parked himself in front of the crease, I took a two-handed whack at the back of his ankles with my stick. I didn't break anything, but it did put him out of that game. I guess it's forgotten, because I've played golf with him since then and he seemed pretty friendly.

It wasn't fun when the Boston fans threw bottles and other stuff at me when I went out for warmups. And it wasn't fun when I got sent back down to the minors in Oklahoma City.

It was no fun when I was put on the expansion list when the Flyers came into the league and they took me and Doug Favell, another young goalie.

It was no fun when the Flyers traded me to Toronto right after I'd gotten married and we'd bought a house in New Jersey. I cried real tears. It turned out to be a good thing because Jacques Plante, my boyhood hero, was the goalie in Toronto. He taught me things about angles and balance and preparation.

I was playing without a signed contract in Toronto when the World Hockey Association was organized, and they came around with an offer I couldn't refuse. It was for more money in one year than I would have made in five in Toronto.

I thought I was going to Miami, and I might have the only Screaming Eagle jersey in existence. But right after I signed, they shifted that franchise to Philadelphia and I was a Blazer. Opening night was Friday the 13th. Who starts a brand-new league on Friday the 13th? Not that I'm superstitious—it's bad luck to be superstitious.

Anyway, the ice cracked and the fans threw the souvenir orange Blazers pucks at us, real rubber pucks, not the sponge things people collect as souvenirs now.

They brought Derek Sanderson out to explain that the game was postponed because the ice had cracked, and he said, "This is a first. Philadelphia has suffered a first here."

Sanderson was a pretty good hockey player with a lot of charisma. But saying the right thing at the right time was not one of his best skills.

The fans threw more pucks and Sanderson said, "Please come back, we need your support after we get this bloody ice fixed. I hope you can get out of the building. The parking situation isn't that great."

A lot of people don't know this, but Ed Snider, who owned the Flyers, offered the Blazers the Spectrum for the next day, but they refused the offer.

They fixed the ice, we finally played the game, and we lost it. Lost the next six games, too. Sanderson wound up with a herniated disc in his back, and I broke a bone in my foot stopping a shot.

It didn't get much better. It was no fun facing 55 shots a night in a league that was run-and-gun. And then the paychecks stopped coming on time. My agent was worried that they were going to move the team out west somewhere and he didn't want to chase them all over North America to get my money.

His instincts were right. They eventually moved the team to Vancouver. He warned them to pay me what they owed me. The general manager said he didn't negotiate with a gun to his head. They didn't listen, so I bailed out.

The Blazers were in the playoffs at the time, so I caught plenty of heat. But there are times when you have to do what you think is right, and that was one of those times.

Someone asked me how it felt to jump ship during the playoffs, and I said, "I'm a good swimmer."

Handling tough questions with smart-aleck answers—maybe that explains why people thought I was some kind of joker. I may have contributed to that image by talking about what I did on game days. I ate a big steak, a porterhouse, 16 ounces, medium rare, with 10 mushrooms—*exactly* 10 mushrooms.

I'm not sure why. Then I'd take a nap with Tinker Bell, wake up, and watch The Three Stooges on television. Hey, you've got to admit, those guys were funny.

I just believed that if you were happy and in a good mood, that carried over when you got to the rink. I'd joke with the guys in the room, make small talk, brag about my hunting or fishing. I'd tell 'em about Tinker Bell and The Three Stooges, loosen the mood. Sometimes guys would ask me, "How many goals are we gonna need tonight?" And I would say, "One!"

And some nights, I'd say, "Two." They'd ask The Chief, Bobby Taylor, when he was in goal, and he would say, "Ten!" Different guys handle pressure differently.

Playing goalie in the National Hockey League was never fun. What was it like? The best way to describe it is to say it was like living on the edge, all the time. It was like walking on the edge of a cliff, 1,000 feet high. Sure, I enjoyed the preparation the night before a game. I enjoyed practice, learning new things. But on game days, from the moment I woke up from my nap, it was hell.

Those hours from 3:00 PM until the game ended were brutal. People think you're doing something you love, so it must be neat. You're happy with God-given talent, but even if you're well prepared and you have a good warmup, once the game starts, you can't control the outcome.

You start out playing well, and then the other team gets a 5-on-3, scores a couple of goals, and the momentum swings. You're the goalie, so there's nobody behind you. Make a mistake, no one can rescue you. The red light goes on.

I remember that Flyers head coach (and later the team's general manager) Keith Allen once said, "Bernie always talked about the pressure, but he seemed immune to it."

If that's what people want to remember, that's okay. But what they don't realize is how much preparation I did the night before the game. I'd study films, I'd look for clues, who was left-handed, who was right-handed, which foot they shot off, how my defensemen handled different guys.

Anticipation was such a big part of my game. Focus. I had my own system, and it demanded I not let up for an instant. Relax for a second and the puck could wind up behind me.

Every game was like a war. Tough, intense, physical.

And there were times in a tight game where I'd say some things that made people think I was a little flakey. Okay, a *lot* flakey. Like the time I skated up to Eddie Van Impe during a scoreless playoff game and said, "I don't know whether I'm gonna have one piece of pizza after the game, or two."

If you look at the films of the last game of the 1974 Stanley Cup Finals against Boston, there were a few seconds left as I skated up to Joe Watson. "Joe," I said, "if we win tonight we're gonna have women lined up outside our door every day this summer." We called Joe "Thundermouth," and he was loud and easy to rile up. He started screaming at me, asking if I knew where we were, if I knew what was at stake. And I just laughed.

Which was a little different from the message our coach, Freddie Shero, wrote on the blackboard before the final game the first time we won the Cup. He wrote, "Win tonight and we walk together forever." He was right, and that's why so many guys from that team still live near Philadelphia, still get together for old-timer nights, still don't have to pay for a drink or dinner. It's one of the reasons 45,000 people showed up at Citizens Bank Park to watch the Flyers alumni play the Rangers alumni on New Year's Eve 2011.

We never got to skate the Cup around the rink for a victory lap the day we won it. The fans at the Spectrum had scrambled out of their seats and they were all over the ice, along with photographers. So we lugged the big silver Cup back to the dressing room and sipped champagne out of it.

We didn't spray the stuff at each other. I don't remember having champagne in the room for that. It was mainly beer. And pretty soon the room got crowded with friends and relatives.

The parade should have been fun, but it turned crazy. The players were in convertibles and the fans on the sidewalks kept dodging the cops to come up to the cars with beers and handshakes. It got so wild, somebody threw a beer can and hit Bobby Clarke on his sore leg. They grabbed at him, and finally, Clarke and his wife had to leave the parade.

They ripped a sleeve off Don Saleski's sports jacket, and when we got to the end of the parade, he stood up there, with one sleeve torn off, and one of the guys said, "If he sues for damages, he might get four bucks."

Philadelphia teams hadn't won many championships, so this was the first real big parade, and the fans didn't know how to act. Sure, we were a bunch of Canadians, with a lot of missing teeth. Most of us came from really small towns and grew up playing in front of small crowds in small arenas. Most of us lived in New Jersey and talked funny, eh? But we had charisma, the fans could see our faces, and they loved the way we played, especially when we became the Broad Street Bullies. We were a blue-collar team in a blue-collar town.

The combination of excitement and beer got to me. I needed to take a pit stop, so I jumped out of the car. They tell me it was somewhere in the 1500 block on Broad Street. Six cops surrounded me and one of the cops put handcuffs on me so I wouldn't get kidnapped, I guess. Or wander off.

They hustled me to somebody's house in South Philadelphia so I could use the bathroom. The family was thrilled. I understand they took that toilet and bronzed it. I'm not sure there's ever been more publicity about some guy taking a pee, unless the guy got arrested afterward.

When we won the Cup again in 1975, everybody was better prepared. They put the players on flat-bed trucks so the fans couldn't paw at us. I was standing next to Frank Rizzo at the start.

He was police commissioner first and then got elected mayor. He was tough, a real man's man. I loved Frank Rizzo. He kept staring at the rooftops as we rode down Broad Street.

Finally, I got up the courage to ask him what he was looking for. He said, "Snipers!" I gulped and then I said to myself, "See ya, big guy, you're on your own" and I moved to the back of the float.

We got to the end of the parade, and when it was my turn to speak, I said, "We'll see you here again next May 27th."

I don't think I jinxed us. It was just something I truly believed. I thought we would win it again the next year. But it didn't happen and hasn't happened since, although the Flyers have come close a couple of times.

I got hurt the next year and hardly played. I had to have surgery on my neck. Two years later, Jimmy Watson was trying to shove Don Maloney of the Rangers out of the crease and his stick came up and poked through my mask and slashed my right eye.

Bam! In an instant, my career was over.

They led me off the ice with blood gushing down my face. The tendons had been slashed. They couldn't save the vision in that eye. The next morning I was completely blind, because the shock had caused me to lose vision in the other eye.

I officially retired on June 1, 1979. I understand now that everything in this life that happens to you, even the bad things, is for a reason.

I wasn't prepared for life after hockey, not physically, not emotionally. I sank into depression. I looked for answers in the bottom of beer bottles. I'd look into the mirror and ask myself, who was this person? I was no longer a hockey player, and that was all I knew how to do.

It didn't help that my agent had squandered my money on bad investments. It didn't help that my marriage unraveled. I retreated to my boat, because it offered a refuge, a peaceful place.

I made sure my wife and kids could continue to live the same lifestyle they were accustomed to. Me, I ran out of money, and couldn't make the payments on the boat, *The French Connection*. It was repossessed.

I drank too much and partied too hard. My wife, Carol, was worried. She had handed me a questionnaire, 25 questions. If you answered three of them in the affirmative, there was a chance you were an alcoholic. Twenty-five questions, and I had the wrong answer on 24 of them. The 25th question, I lied a little. A few days later I went out and drank too much. Suddenly, I thought about that questionnaire.

I made a phone call, asking for help. And then I stopped, cold. I found the help I needed. I haven't had a drink in more than 31 years.

I had rented an apartment and lived on peanut butter and jelly sandwiches for a stretch. One morning I came downstairs to find a bunch of people sprawled around the place, sleeping, too hung over to go home.

I stepped over one and at that point I said, "Enough! I'm never gonna be in this situation again." I joined a self-help program and got the support I needed.

It's been a fascinating journey, from the mountaintops of success to the swamps of despair. I never, ever thought of quitting, not even when the fans in Boston were throwing stuff at me.

Getting traded by the Flyers to Toronto in 1971 had me crying like a baby. But my idol, Jacques Plante, was still playing for the Leafs, and he taught me so much about the game that the trade turned out to be a blessing.

I jumped to the WHA and that was a nightmare, facing 50 shots a game in front of small crowds in bad arenas amid broken promises. But I learned from that, too. I left the Blazers during the playoffs because they didn't live up to an agreement, and somehow I did not worry about a backlash from the NHL.

I came back to the Philadelphia Flyers and had incredible success, winning two Vezina

Trophies, two Conn Smythe Trophies as most valuable player in the playoffs, plus a car that I gave away to Freddie. But none of the individual awards meant anything compared to the back-to-back Stanley Cups we won.

And then the stick in the eye, the blood on the ice, total darkness for a week, and realizing that my career was over. I was not prepared. Depression followed the darkness. Excessive drinking followed the depression.

Would a therapist have helped along the way? Would professional guidance have helped? People ask me to look back and wonder out loud if a psychiatrist could have eased some of the pain along the way.

I answer those questions with a brief story about Freddie Shero and the time he thought a psychologist could help our hockey team. I was sitting at my locker at the end of the room, and here comes Freddie walking through the door with a stranger.

There had been rumors about Freddie bringing in a shrink. I screamed at the guy, "Get out of here!" Freddie put his finger on his nose and pushed his glasses back, which was something he did often when he needed a moment to figure out what he wanted to say or do next.

The guy was stunned and turned around and walked away, alongside Freddie. We never saw him again. I don't know if Freddie found him in Canada or in New York or sat down next to him in a bar and thought he could help us.

That was 30-something years ago. There didn't seem to be a place for a shrink in hockey. That was the culture. If you had a problem, you talked to teammates, the trainer, maybe the coach. Not some shrink!

And we were the Broad Street Bullies! How would it have looked if the Broad Street Bullies, as tough as we were, needed a shrink? No way!

"ABOVE THE EYEBROWS, ABOVE THE FRAY"

Bernie had problems explaining his philosophy of goaltending. Perhaps he wanted to keep the opposition guessing, perhaps he wasn't sure of what it was himself. So much of his style was based on preparation and anticipation, and that ran counter to the "some fun, eh?" image he cultivated. (Originally published in the Philadelphia Daily News, *April 27, 1978)*

"The mind," Bernie Parent said, "is like the body. You don't exercise it, it can go sour."

The mind? For years we figured if you peered inside Parent's head you'd find a six-pack, a puppy dog, a fishing boat, and a school of tuna.

Now, Jacques Plante comes around, telling us the most important part of a goaltender is from the eyebrows up. And now, Parent sits there, saying, "Losing a game doesn't make you less of a human being."

What kind of calisthenics has Parent been doing above the eyebrows? Is he playing so brilliantly lately because he finally understands that a soft goal or a hard defeat do not diminish him as a man?

"It comes from experience," Parent said the other night, after another splendid performance against Buffalo. "Plus I've been reading a lot. Mostly Wayne Dwyer. He wrote *Erroneous Zones*. And he's come up with a new book called *Pulling Your Own String*. The kind of books you don't just depend on.

"You make up your own mind. You take whatever fits your philosophy. The thing is, I communicate much more now than I used to.

"I'm a great believer in communication. The more you have, the better off you're gonna be."

For years, Parent kept his thoughts bottled inside him while standing upright in the harsh glare a goalie carried around with him like an aura.

Wine turns to vinegar if you store it upright, in a bottle that is not absolutely air-tight, in harsh glare of any kind.

"Let me give you an example," he said. "You're 28 years old. You play a bad game. So, you put those 28 years into that one bad game and you consider yourself a reject.

"That doesn't make sense."

Parent had to wrestle the demons of injury of bad investments, of red lights blinking behind him. Life had turned into one long series of small craft warnings.

Then they showed filums (that's what Shero called them) of the Stanley Cup victories. Parent had some golden memories to cherish, some triumphs to remember, some calm seas full of fish yearning to be caught.

And then Plante returned to Philadelphia to talk softly with Parent. Not just about Xs and Os, but about all 26 letters of the alphabet.

"We talk about a lot of things," Plante said. "He makes a mistake, lets in a bad goal, he knows what he did wrong. We don't have to talk about that.

"The guy is a standup goalie. If you're staying back, you're gonna have more room open. Then you have to throw yourself down. You give up the rebound, and that's how they score on you."

There in 40 words or less is the essence of Parent's goaltending. Stand up, come out to cut down the angles, use your body as part of the equation in the rink's geometry, blotting out the danger zones. The erroneous zones?

"He senses now," Plante said, trying to explain Parent's current groove. "If you wait until the puck has left the stick, it's too late.

"You [react] with the motion. As the motion is made, Bernie's on his way. He's more alert like this."

Parent is agile, mobile, hostile once again, trundling away from the doorstep to chase down pucks, smother them, bat them away.

"He's controlling the puck in our end," said Bobby Clarke. "That's why there's so few rebounds."

Fred Shero measures Parent's self-assurance by the yard. "He wouldn't be gambling for the puck, challenging for it, if he didn't have confidence."

Confidence is a word Parent dreads, like a 3-on-1 break. "A very vicious word," Parent said. "You can have confidence for five minutes and then, *whoosh*, lose it for five minutes.

"I'd rather stay with the word *concentration*. If you know what you're doing, and you concentrate on what you're doing, confidence has nothing to do with it.

"Make a mistake and you keep on concentrating on the game, you forget that mistake."

Parent knows what he's doing. He seems to have that unblinking concentration back, able to survive the strung-out, three-hour scenario that is televised playoff hockey.

He has played seven consecutive playoff games, so his body is thoroughly exercised. His mind is sharp, too. He has Plante to communicate with so his thoughts are spilling out, bubbling, lively.

Like champagne?

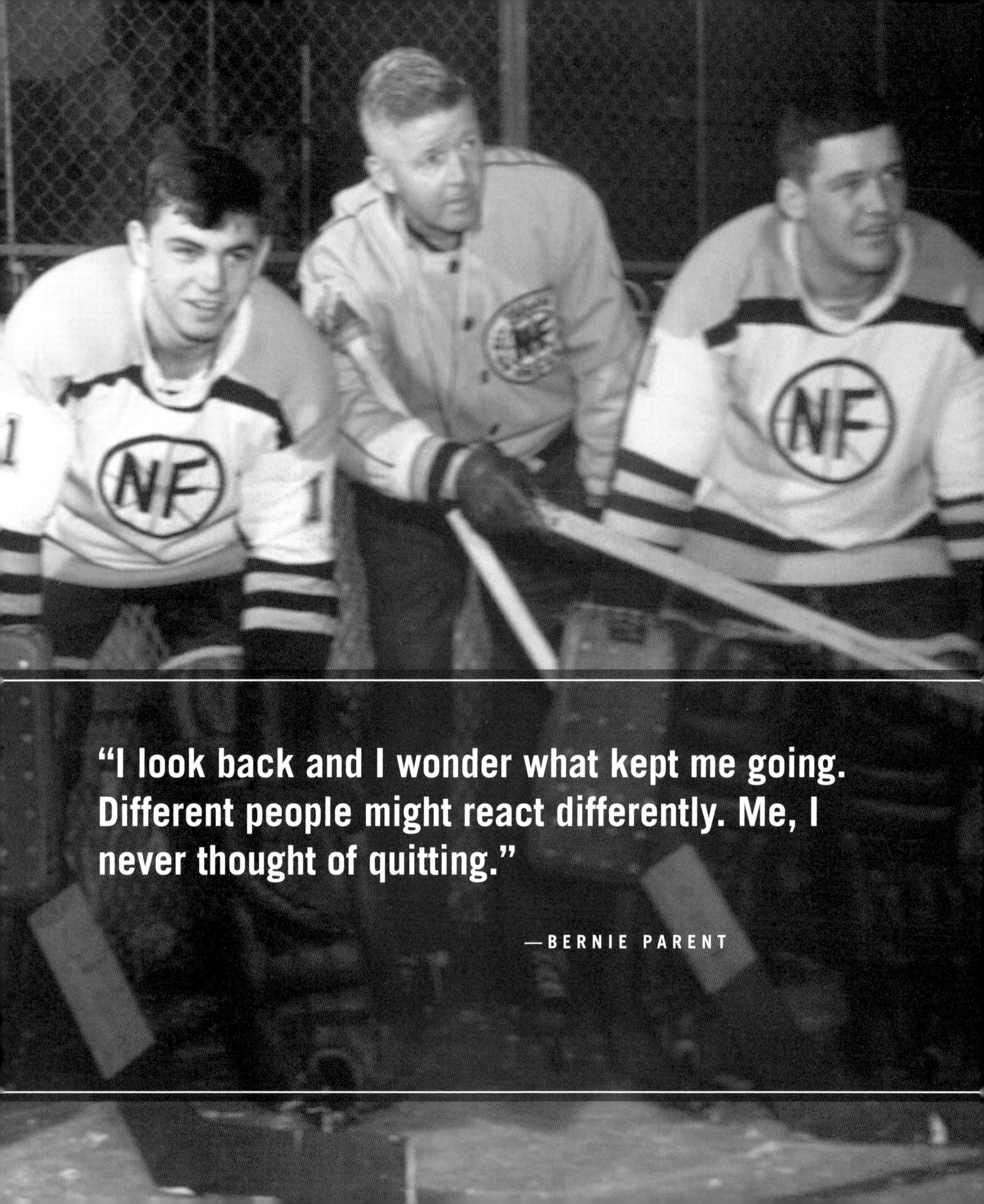

"I look back and I wonder what kept me going. Different people might react differently. Me, I never thought of quitting."

—BERNIE PARENT

HOCKEY NIGHT, BATH NIGHT

I remember being scared of the dark as a kid, which doesn't sound like a great start for someone who wound up being a goalie.

I don't remember standing out in the middle of the street when I was three years old, holding up my hand, stopping traffic. I don't remember the truck drivers climbing down out of their trucks, lifting me up by the armpits, and putting me back on the sidewalk, where I belonged.

Fearlessly playing traffic cop—that's a better story, and some people have printed that story, but I can't remember doing that. I do remember being scared of the dark.

And, as long as I'm confessing to fears, I dread airplane rides. And I'm not that happy riding a bus, either.

I was born on April 3, 1945, in Quebec, the youngest of Claude and Emilie Parent's seven children. My mother had been sick with pneumonia before I was born, so I got off to a rocky start.

My two brothers and four sisters were a lot older than me. We had a good relationship, but I was always aware of the age difference. I guess I became a loner, a maverick, doing my own thing, with a mind of my own, not depending on other people.

What I do remember is being six or seven years old and watching *Hockey Night in Canada*. That was on Saturday night, which was also bath night. My father worked for the Canada Cement Company and we didn't have a lot of money, so we bathed once a week, on Saturdays.

Christmas would come, and we didn't get a lot of gifts. What I remember is gathering around the tree, singing songs. I look back on that, and it seems beautiful.

I grew up in Rosemont, in east Montreal. I was an outdoors kid. When I started playing hockey, it was my mother who came to the games to support me. My father taught me to hunt and fish. To this day I love being outdoors.

Watching* Hockey Night in Canada, *that's when you first realize the importance of winning a Stanley Cup.

I watched a game when I was a kid, the Canadiens against Chicago, and they played and played until it was almost 2:00 in the morning. It was a tremendous thing. I wondered what it would feel like to play for the Cup.

I played all kinds of sports growing up—baseball, football, hockey. I soon found out I wasn't fast enough to play shortstop. We'd play hockey in the streets because it stayed cold a long time and the ice didn't melt.

I think I was 12 before I played in an organized league. My parents had bought me skates, but they were regulation skates, not goalie skates, which they couldn't afford.

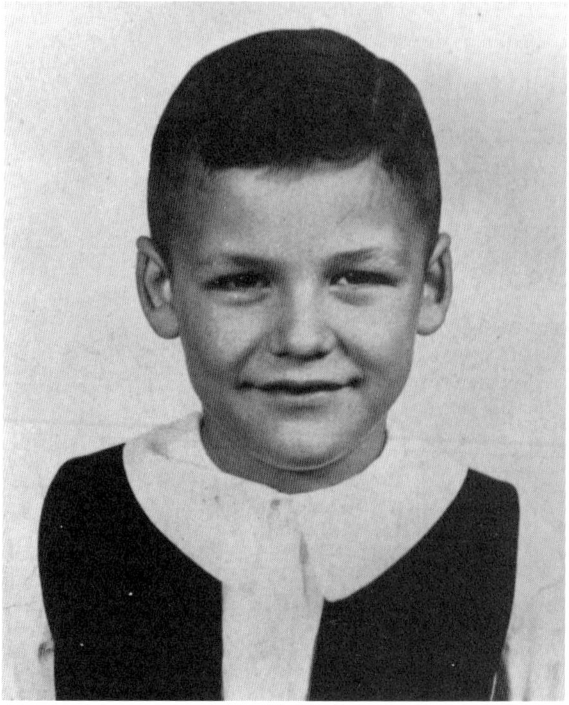

The coach had everybody skate around the rink while he timed us with a stopwatch. And then he'd say "forward" or "defenseman" depending on how fast we were. The average time was 14 seconds. I took 21 seconds to get around. He said, "Goalie."

I gave up 21 goals the first game I played. He said, "Gone!"

I can't really blame it on the skates. I just didn't know what I was doing, and I didn't have good balance. But the next kid they tried got hurt, and before you knew it, I was back in goal. My brother, Yvan, who later became a child psychologist, coached the team.

The writers thought that was funny, a goalie with a brother who was a psychologist. I told them that we talked all the time and that I used to drive him crazy, that he'd have to go to a shrink himself. I did buy him a couch one year, a really good couch. And he did say I had a strong mind that helped me deal with adversity.

I grew up idolizing Jacques Plante and I loved watching him play.

Even as a kid, I could sense him trying to outthink the shooter. I loved his style, and I was fascinated by the way he handled himself. We'd go out to play street hockey and I always pretended to be Plante. The other kids, they picked forwards and centers to emulate. They tried to copy their moves and styles. Me, I was always Plante.

I GREW UP IN ROSEMONT, IN EAST MONTREAL. I WAS AN OUTDOORS KID. WHEN I STARTED PLAYING HOCKEY, IT WAS MY MOTHER WHO CAME TO THE GAMES TO SUPPORT ME. MY FATHER TAUGHT ME TO HUNT AND FISH.

—BERNIE PARENT

Believe it or not, Plante's sister Therese lived next door to us. He would come to visit and we'd hide in the bushes to get a look at him.

He loved to smoke cigars, which probably explains why I love to smoke cigars. And now, after Flyers home games at the Wells Fargo Center in South Philadelphia, I mingle with the fans in the Holt's Cigar lounge and I smoke $12 cigars. People look at me funny when I tell them that. They want to know if I can tell the difference between a $2 cigar and a $12 cigar. What difference does it make, they ask, since it all goes up in smoke anyway? I tell them that it's like people who really enjoy wine and talk about color, aroma, and taste. Well, with a good cigar, the color is right because the tobacco is really good tobacco. And you can sniff it and tell by the smell that it's really good tobacco.

You light it up and the aroma is there; you can feel the difference in a really good cigar. And I confess, I do like the finer things in life. But that's getting way ahead of the story.

I was a lousy student, even though one of my sisters was a schoolteacher. Even at a young age, I hated being told what to do.

Schoolwork was boring and seemed to have no purpose. My mind would wander. It was like I was going in circles, with no destination and nothing to show for it. In hockey, I had a purpose: I had the Stanley Cup to shoot for.

As it turns out, I played junior hockey for one of the two Montreal teams that the Canadiens did not sponsor. So there went the dreams of playing for Montreal. I signed with Boston, and they sent me off to play for Niagara Falls in the Ontario Hockey Association. The Niagara Falls *Flyers*, can you believe that? I was 16 years old. All we spoke around the house was French. All we spoke in school was French. All we spoke in the streets was French. I only knew a handful of English words.

My parents took me to the train station in Montreal for the trip to Niagara Falls. I met Gilles Marotte at the station. My biggest worry was the language barrier. Marotte was from Virden, knew some English, and he said he

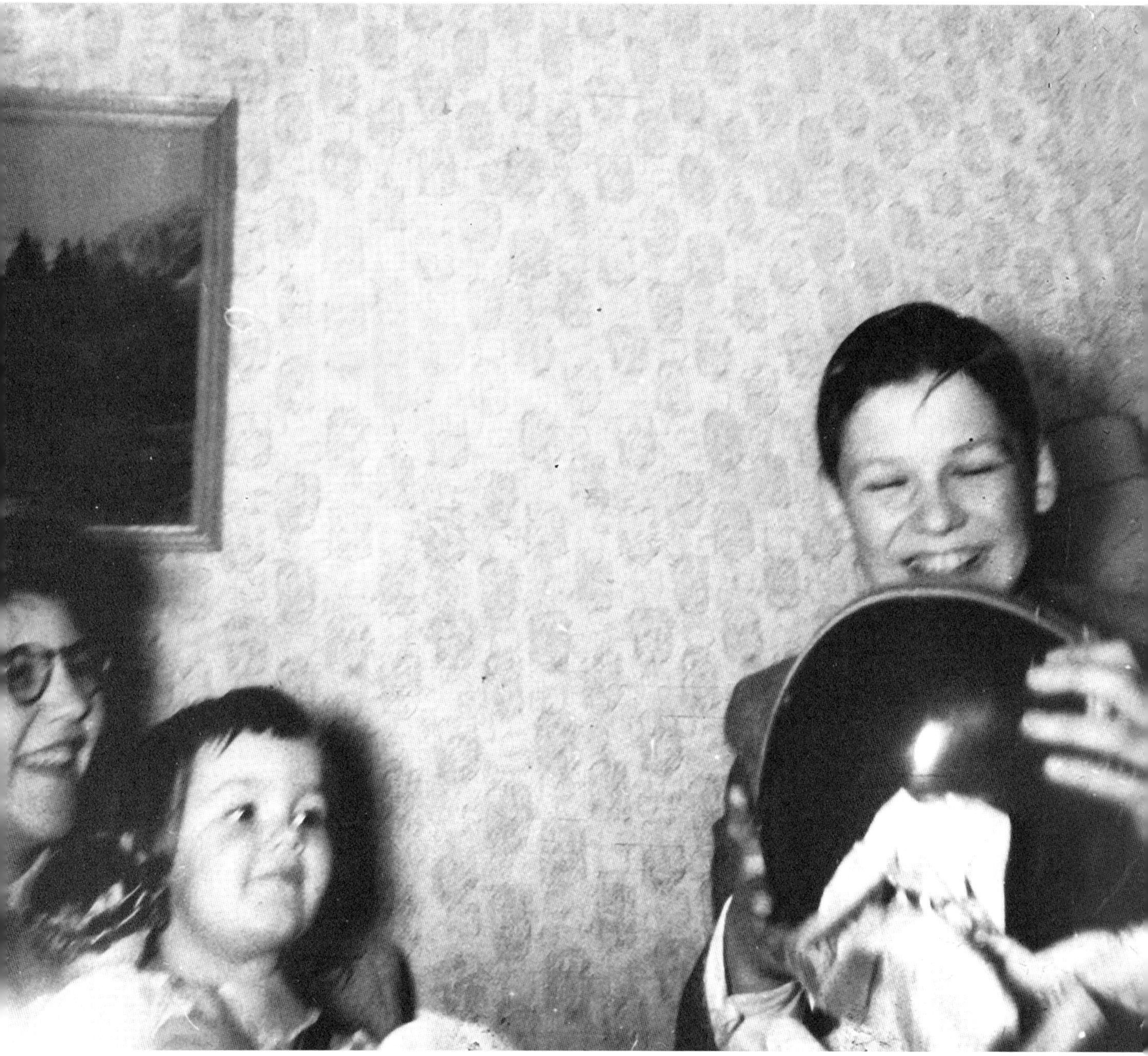

SCHOOLWORK WAS BORING

AND SEEMED TO HAVE NO PURPOSE....

IN HOCKEY, I HAD A PURPOSE:

I HAD THE STANLEY CUP TO SHOOT FOR.

—BERNIE PARENT

would help me, but I couldn't imagine being with him every minute of the day.

My stomach was churning the whole trip, wondering what Niagara Falls and my teammates would be like.

Harold Cotton, a Boston scout, was there to meet us when we got off the train. I remember he had two gold teeth and he was smoking a big, fat cigar. He said, "So, you're Parent." And then he started talking a mile a minute and I didn't understand a word he was saying.

I almost turned around and got back on the train. We took a cab to the rink and that's when we met Hap Emms, who owned the team. Emms was a very disciplined person, by which I mean he was really tough.

He was the right guy for young players who needed to learn discipline and good work habits. Sure, there were times when I really got angry at him, but looking back, he really helped me get better as a player. We had a bunch of guys on our team who went on to have good careers, including Derek Sanderson, Doug Favell, Bill Goldsworthy, John Arbour, and Brian Bradley.

Some of his rules seemed strange. He wouldn't let us shoot pool, eat hot dogs, or order ice cream, for example. I'm not sure why he banned ice cream. Maybe he thought it was bad for us, or maybe he was just watching his expenses.

Bill Long was the coach, and he had a softer side than Emms. Still, my first year was a very difficult one. Communication was tough. I couldn't understand Long and he couldn't understand me. I wound up going to school to learn English, but I struggled. I lasted maybe two months before I got bored and moved on.

By then I had picked up enough of the language to communicate with people. The people who lived there were wonderful and willing to help. It's not like I couldn't order food in a restaurant—not that it mattered much, because we didn't go to restaurants often. Meal money was practically nonexistent. We got $5 a week. If we stayed at the Harrison hotel, the meals were paid for by the team. If we went out on our own, hey, *café* is *coffee* in English, you figure out the rest. Sure, I made a lot of mistakes trying to speak the language, but people were kind.

I got off to such an incredibly bad start on the ice. I didn't have my equipment. The Rosemont team had refused to release it. I guess they wanted money, and Emms was too cheap or too stubborn to pay for it. That went on for two months. I couldn't play; I couldn't even practice. I'd travel with the team but I couldn't be part of it. Here I am, a kid who couldn't speak the language, couldn't play, and couldn't show what I could do. Finally, my dad, a guy with seven kids making an average middle-class salary, had to come up with the money to buy the equipment and send it to me.

I look back and I wonder what kept me going. Different people might react differently. Me, I never thought of quitting.

I never thought about failure. Besides, how do you define failure? If you're trying hard and you don't succeed, you're not failing—you're just creating a result. Even as a young kid, quitting was never part of my vocabulary.

Bill Long really helped me. I had no concept of how important angles were in playing goal. I'd heard people talk about them, but I didn't understand. I knew how to stop the puck, but I didn't understand how to make it tougher on the shooter. Long used ropes to show me. That's right—he took a 20-foot rope, wrapped it around my waist, and then attached one end to each goal post. If I came straight out of the goal the rope would stretch like a V. If I moved to one side or the other, the rope would stretch in

IT WAS IN NIAGARA FALLS THAT I FIRST BECAME AWARE OF THE MAGIC IN THE DRESSING ROOM. I DIDN'T DEVELOP SOCIALIZING SKILLS AS A YOUNGSTER. THAT CAME MUCH LATER ON.

—BERNIE PARENT

a different way, and when I looked back I could see that the shooter had less of the net to shoot at. After that, I had a better understanding of the angles, and that became a vital part of my game. I was now an angle goalie. I was also a standup goalie. Back in those days you hardly had anybody who flopped.

I had a decent year that first season, and made second-team OHA. Chuck Goddard of Peterborough was first team. I was near the top of the leaderboard in goals-against average, which is not too shabby in a league that included scorers like Yvan Cournoyer, Pete Stemkowski, Dennis Hull, and Ron Buchanan. Bobby Orr was just getting started, along with guys like Doug Jarrett, Ken Hodge, and Mike Walton.

It was in Niagara Falls that I first became aware of the magic in the dressing room. I didn't develop socializing skills as a youngster. That came much later on. There are only a few people in that room, so that makes you part of a special club, not just a team. There's a mystique and respect in that room. The fun we had, the togetherness we shared, that was special for me. I look back on a time when I could barely speak the language and I didn't have my equipment, and I am so grateful that the guys in that room became my family. When that happens, life takes a funny shape. Suddenly you win as a family, you cry after losses as a family, and you support each other.

The next season, we had an even better team. We'd added Jean Pronovost and Rosey Paiement. At that time, Montreal was in the OHA, and it was exciting to play in the Forum because I had grown up nearby. We finished first that season. The fans picked me as the most valuable player. I had a 2.51 goals-against average, lowest in the league. We won the Memorial Cup, beating Edmonton in a series that included an amazing brawl.

It started when Sanderson sucker punched Bob Falkenberg, and then all hell broke loose as fans jumped on the ice. I remember Emms saying afterward, "This isn't hockey, it's war."

I soon realized I had the toughest job in sports. In baseball, a pitcher throws a pitch, and unless the guy hits it out of the park for a home run, the pitcher has a lot of people behind him to make plays. In football, if the quarterback throws a bad pass and it gets intercepted, he's still got 10 other guys out there to make the tackle, to save a touchdown.

When a goalie makes a mistake, there's nobody behind him. The puck goes in the net, and the red light goes on.

I do think pitchers and quarterbacks get too much credit when their teams win and too much blame when their teams lose. In hockey, you have five other guys out there with you. Each guy has a job to do. When the team plays well, it helps the goalie play well. If the team doesn't play well in front of you, there's a pretty good chance you will not play well.

There's no in-between. You have to get used to being criticized when you lose. It comes with the territory. A goalie needs a short memory and a thick skin.

Boston called me up after we won the Memorial Cup. They didn't put a lot of pressure on me—they just wanted me to be the guy who turned the Bruins into a playoff contender when they'd been finishing at the bottom for years. No sweat.

As it happened, that year was the first time in six seasons they did not finish last.

Let's face it, I was young, undisciplined, and my practice habits were not what they should have been. All that showed in games.

One night in Boston, the starting goalie, Ed Johnston, got cut on his forehead. I stepped on the ice to replace him, and *bang*, the fans were throwing bottles at me. You don't get bottles thrown at you if you've been playing well. So I probably deserved that treatment.

I got sent down to Oklahoma City. Marcel Pelletier, who worked for the Flyers, saw me there and liked what he saw. I'm not exactly sure what caught his eye. Maybe because we were both Frenchmen? Maybe he needed glasses? Whatever it was, he was a goalie when he played, and he understood the position and filed a good report on me. Next stop: Philadelphia.

"PARENT DREAMS OF CUP SWEEP"

There is some ominous foreshadowing in this column. Bernie talked about playing seven or eight more years. But a horrible eye injury ended his career sadly, suddenly. He was not prepared for life after hockey. (Originally published in the Philadelphia Daily News, *April 22, 1975)*

On his birthday, Bernie Parent played well and the Flyers tied the Rangers 1–1 in a bitter, furious game. Afterward, a man asked Parent if there was any pattern…did he often have memorable games on his birthday?

Parent hesitated for about four awkward seconds. "I guess," he said, "the best birthday I ever had…was the day I was born."

"Oh," said the man, caught up helplessly in the gag. "How many saves did you get THAT day?"

"One," Parent said swiftly. "I saved my mother some more aggravation."

Once he skates onto the ice, Parent never removes his stark white fiberglass mask. People think it hides a quivering lip or some other telltale tic of tension. Does it?

"I am," Parent said, with no pause at all, "like Elvis Presley. I cannot go out there if one hair is messed and out of place."

And when the game is over, the fiberglass mask is replaced by an invisible shield, just as tough, just as protective. Parent will not endure more than one serious question a night.

The second one chases him on some quixotic errand around the clubhouse….back into the shower, in search of a clean towel, onto the scale to weigh himself. Again.

Or, he will stand there and duck behind that invisible mask, with the invisible jester's smile on it. Will the real Bernie Parent please stand up? The guy who hides the pregame jitters behind paint and plastic…or the guy who wraps his postgame thoughts in jokes?

"I guess," Parent said, "nobody has stood up yet."

It was tantalizing enough, waiting for the real Bernie Parent to stand up. Now, we have another dimension to the mystery, wondering how a fat new contract calling for yearly payments for the rest of his life will affect the world's greatest goaltender.

"It has affected many in sports," Fred Shero said ominously. "You see people get long-term contracts and it destroys them as athletes. They never give you the same again.

"But the real stars work harder. Guys like Bobby Clarke and Parent, they know no other way to play. They just play their best. Very few should be superstars. The rest can't take it."

Put a pot of gold at the end of a rainbow, some guys are going to take short cuts to get there. Parent must play six more years to earn that guaranteed yearly income. He will be 36 then. That seems very young.

"I can see him playing until he's 40," said club president Ed Snider. "He's got the greatest temperament of any goalie I've ever seen. He's smooth, with an even disposition. He's a beautiful guy."

Nerves tend to unravel before the eyesight blurs or the legs wobble. "If Jacques Plante can play til he's 44, Bernie can play until he's

40," said personnel director Marcel Pelletier. "Bernie's nerves are 100 percent better now. He used to be a nervous kid, uncertain.

"Now, he believes in himself. All the great ones do. He has no fear. And he doesn't abuse himself when he plays. He stands up."

It seems frivolous to worry about how long Parent will play, while the Flyers are elbow-deep in the Stanley Cup playoffs. At least, it seems that way to Clarke, the soul of this team.

"It's the wrong time to talk about lifetime contracts," Clarke said. "Besides, I'm in the middle of a long-term contract I'm happy with. What have I got to go? Five more years?

"It's wrong to talk about lifetime contracts. What have we done to deserve that kind of contract?"

Clarke frets about the players will think. Does he worry at all what the fans might say if Parent plays poorly? "He won't ever play bad," Clarke said. "He's a much better goalie now than four years ago, and then, he didn't play bad.

"If he had to face 40 shots a night, he might feel different [about early retirement]. Same with me. If I played for a team like Washington and got beat 8–1 or 9–2 night after night, I'd look for something else. When you've been on top it's tough to adjust to that.

"You have to look at the whole team. It's easier for Bernie, because he's got a good team in front of him. The other team has to shoot from further out, from tougher angles."

Parent knows this and he never hesitates to talk about it. "We've got a good hockey club," he said, "and it should be good for a lot of years. I can see myself playing seven or eight more years.

"You can't be a robot. You've got to learn from your mistakes. On the ice. And off the ice. I like to be around the guys. I love the game. And most of all, I love to win."

The Flyers won the quarterfinal match with Toronto 4–0. A 12-game sweep to the Stanley Cup is still possible. "I dreamed that," Parent confessed. "I dreamed we won 12 straight."

Oh, the man asked sheepishly, does Parent dream often? Do his dreams usually come true?

"Nahhhh," said Bernie, "I usually wake up before I get the broad."

“I understood why Philadelphia made the trade. The Flyers needed offense, and they had to trade a goalie to get scoring.”

—BERNIE PARENT

CHAPTER THREE

CHILLY IN PHILLY

They brought six new teams into the NHL in 1967 and stuck them all in one division, which seemed fair. The Original Six teams got to protect certain players on their rosters, and the expansion teams got to pick players from the unprotected list.

Los Angeles had the first pick in the expansion draft and selected goalie Terry Sawchuk, who had just taken Toronto to the Stanley Cup. That left lots of established goalies available, including Glenn Hall, Charlie Hodge, and Ed Johnston. Boston wanted to protect Gerry Cheevers. I was 22, and Cheevers was 25. They figured some team would pick Johnston, even though he was 10 years older than me, because I didn't have a great second season for the Bruins. In the days of the Original Six you played each other over and over. The average age of a hockey player was 27, and there were a lot of smart players in the league. By a player's second year, they got to know your weaknesses. If you didn't have enough experience to overcome those weaknesses, you struggled, and that's what happened to me.

In the end, the Flyers picked me anyway. Boston protected Johnston and the Flyers then also took my buddy, Doug Favell. Bud Poile was the general manager in Philadelphia and he made the picks.

I had a reputation of being a little immature, and maybe I was. Marcel Pelletier was a scout for the Flyers, and he had watched me and liked me. He'd seen me play in Oklahoma City and he said I had the perfect temperament for a goalie: win, lose, or draw, I was always the same. He said I'd go home, have a couple of beers, kiss my wife, and go to sleep. He was an optimist. He said we'd have a young team and he didn't see any reason why we couldn't win the Stanley Cup four or five times in the next 10 years.

Years later, someone told me that right after the expansion draft, Chicago offered the Flyers $250,000 to buy me. I guess the Flyers kept that a secret because they didn't want me getting a big head—or asking for a raise.

At first, they made me the starting goaltender, but then I lost that role to Favell after a bad training camp. Maybe they thought I'd learn from it. I was only two days older than Doug, but we were two very different goalies. Doug was way ahead of his time. He played then the way goalies play today. He was very exciting. I didn't have the flexibility he had, which is why I was a standup goalie. He was cool, but he didn't have a system. That's why he'd be hot for 10 days, and then he'd cool off. It was hard for him to get back on track when he was struggling; after all, if you don't have a system, how do you correct the things that have gone wrong?

I remember Doug being the first one to drink Coke between periods. Yo, it was 1967, and you weren't supposed to drink anything but water. But Doug liked his Coca-Cola. He'd even eat pizza before a game. People thought he was crazy, but I always liked him. In practice, he'd catch pucks between his legs. He'd flop around and make spectacular saves. He was free-spirited, like me. He did his own thing.

The league was hoping for parity when they put all the new teams in the same division, and that's what they got. When the regular season ended, only six points separated the first five teams. We finished first, just barely below .500 at 31–32–11. We were young, with a few older guys sprinkled throughout the roster, such as

Ed Van Impe and Leon Rochefort. We also had some swift little guys to form a "French Line" with Andre Lacroix, Jean-Guy Gendron, and Simon Nolet.

Believe it or not, halfway through the season, Favell and I were leading the Vezina Trophy race; our combined goals-against average was slightly above 2.00. The award money was $250. Can you believe that? I spend that on a box of cigars now.

Just before a scheduled ice show performance in February, the roof blew off the Philadelphia Spectrum—literally. We played the rest of the regular season as a road team, playing our "home" games in Toronto, New York, and Quebec City. So winning the division was quite an accomplishment.

We wound up playing St. Louis in the playoffs. They were big and tough, with guys like the Plager brothers, Barclay and Bob, plus Noel Picard. They'd beat us up, on the ice and on the scoreboard.

We managed to split the first six games. Game 7 was in Philly and St. Louis brought Doug Harvey in to play defense. He was coaching in Kansas City and was around 43 at that time, but he still had enough left to control the pace of the game and even had an assist on the winning goal. That was a tough one to lose.

We took a big step back the next year, finishing a mile behind St. Louis and Oakland. Red Berenson scored six goals in one game against us. Another time we lost 12–0 to Chicago. Both of those games were at the Spectrum in front of stunned crowds. In the playoffs, the Blues pounded us in four straight games. Mr. Snider was really angry, and he told Poile to go out and find some bigger, tougher players.

That partly explains why the Flyers picked Dave Schultz, Don Saleski, and Willie Brossart in the draft. And that was the start of our transformation into the Broad Street Bullies, a nickname pinned on us by Jack Chevalier, a writer for the *Philadelphia Bulletin*.

I got married before my third season in Philly. Belatedly. Carol and I scheduled the wedding for the beginning of the summer in Cherry Hill, New Jersey. My family came down from Montreal. Two days before the wedding, I got cold feet, so I walked away. My family drove back to Montreal.

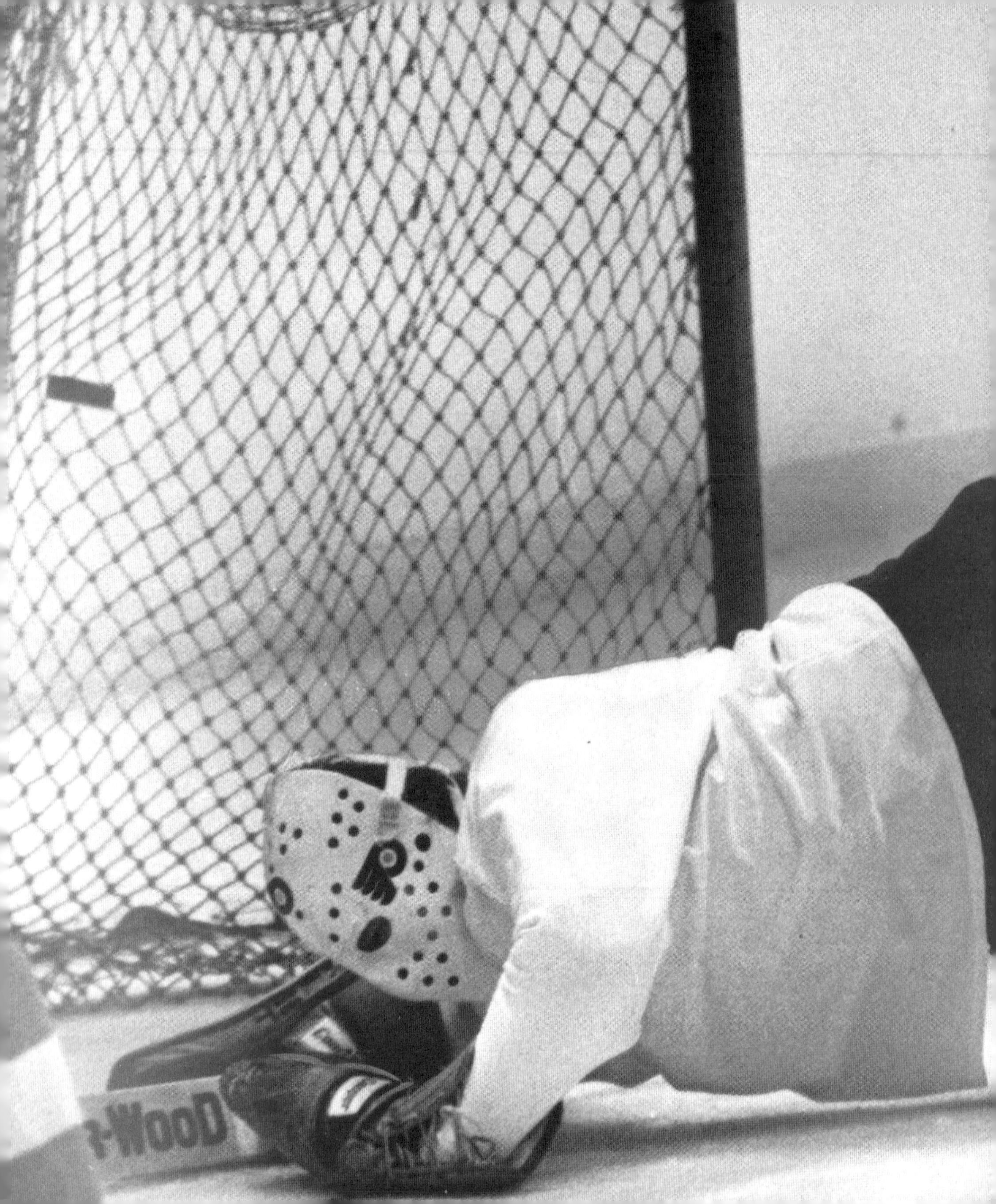

WooD

Cold feet? Pretty soon I had cold hands and a cold nose, because I scooted off to the Canadian Rockies to do some hunting. I have always found peace in the outdoors. When you hunt mule deer at 11,000 feet, you are so concerned about getting your next breath of thin air that you can't be worrying about anything else in your life.

Today I understand why I walked away from the wedding. There's the tremendous force of the wolf inside of me. It had nothing to do with the way I felt toward Carol, because the love was here, no question about it. It's just that at the last minute, I was afraid to lose the wolf within me. The wolf wants his freedom.

When I came back to training camp and saw Carol again, the passion was rekindled. I told my family we were getting married and they said, "Call us when you do, we'll congratulate you over the phone."

So it turned out to be a small wedding, with a justice of the peace in Barrington, Pennsylvania. We bought a house in New Jersey…and then I got traded to Toronto.

I was devastated. Not because we'd just bought a house—when the season ends, you come back home, it's summer time, so that's not a problem. I was worried about my hockey career, and where it was headed.

Keith Allen called me into his office after a game and told me I'd been traded. He said it was the toughest trade he'd ever had to make, that it had taken a lot of soul searching.

He said it was tough from an emotional point of view, because I was a classy kid who had played well for the Flyers. He said you don't want to get too close to the players, but you do, and that's what made it so tough. That was nice, but still no consolation.

I cried like a baby when I got the news. I bumped into Mr. Snider in the corridor at the Spectrum and he started crying, too. There's a picture of the two of us somewhere, tears rolling down our cheeks. Mr. Snider said it was the toughest trade he'd had to approve. But that was his style. He hired people he trusted, and he let them do their thing. If things didn't work out, he'd make some changes, but he allowed his hockey people to make the hockey decisions.

Even Favell was shook up. He said it was a funny feeling—you play with a guy for a long time, and then all of a sudden you're playing

30

with somebody else. He also said he didn't want to play every day because he only weighed 165 pounds. He said he wanted to play, he just didn't think they would break us up.

I understood why Philadelphia made the trade. The Flyers needed offense, and they had to trade a goalie to get scoring.

When I heard the news I was so shook I didn't even ask who I'd been traded for. It wound up being a three-way deal. The Flyers got Mike Walton and Bruce Gamble, a veteran goaltender, plus Toronto's first-round pick in the 1971 draft. They swapped Walton to Boston for Rick MacLeish and Danny Schock. Two years later, MacLeish turned into a 50-goal scorer and a key player on the teams that won the Stanley Cup.

When the trade happened, some fans brought a banner to the Spectrum and hung it from the balcony. It said, "Without a Parent, We're Orphans."

Carol and I were still in shock when we started packing two days later. We got help from Ray Marella, a hunting buddy of mine. We packed everyone in our car, sort of like Noah and the Ark: there were Carol and me; Chuck, her son from a previous marriage; Bernie Jr., who was nine months old; plus our dog Tinker Bell and two gerbils.

We ran into a serious snowstorm near Syracuse, a real blizzard. I thought we'd found a hotel but it was closed because the owner had committed suicide. Twenty miles down the snow-clogged road, we found an open motel. A truck driver told us the roads were clear about 15 miles past Syracuse, so we took off again. I got to Maple Leaf Gardens Wednesday morning in time for the team meeting.

I'm not superstitious and I don't believe in omens. Sure, we'd had a nightmare trip getting to Toronto. But that didn't mean the whole experience was going to be a nightmare. I started feeling good about things the first time I talked to Jacques Plante.

He was 42 and nearing the end of his career. He did not look at me as some young punk trying to take his job. He told me, "We're on the same team, and I can help you."

That's all I wanted to hear. My memories of him went so far back, and he laughed when I told him how we used to watch him from the shrubbery.

I knew he smoked cigars so I bought him some, the best I could find. At that time in Canada, you could buy Cuban cigars, and he appreciated that.

We won a championship when I played in juniors in Montreal. I was lucky that way, playing on a lot of very good teams. At 16, I was using some moves that I had seen Plante use. And I remember him saying, "This kid is going to play in the National Hockey League one day." And then, many years later, here we were, on the same team.

Plante didn't have an outgoing personality; you could say he was a loner. He kept to himself a lot. But I was humble enough to ask for help, and a trust developed between us. He decided that he would help me and he did. He was a great guy, he just didn't like to socialize. If you didn't take the time to understand him, you would think he fell out of a tree somewhere.

He was very disciplined and a very smart goaltender. When I saw him play and I saw how he practiced, I realized that is where I wanted to be.

Plante watched me practice, and the first thing he said was that I had to learn* how *to practice.

I used to be nonchalant in practice. He wanted me to be more disciplined, to develop a system and then stick to it. I had been relying on God-given talent.

He wanted me to have a better understanding of the game, and to apply that in practice. Once I did, my whole career turned around. Spending one year with Plante was like gaining three years of experience. He really taught me how to stand up and play the angles against different shooters. He improved my balance by shifting all my weight onto my right foot, not the left, during a play. He also taught me how to find my exact position by banging my stick or my glove against the posts. I used to take my eyes off the puck to see where I was, and that can cost you a goal.

What I learned most, though, was to anticipate. I'd study the opposition; if a guy was a left-handed shot, I'd study how my defensemen played him. Once I knew that, I'd put myself in position to make the save. If a guy is shooting from the point, he's going to look for an open spot. Put yourself in his mind, cover that opening, get there, and make the save.

I learned early on that it was more fun for the fans to watch the other goalies, the ones with lots of movement. Fans would watch me and say, "This guy is boring to watch. All he does is get hit by shots."

That's anticipation, being in the right spot at the right time. The day before a game, not the day of the game, I'd spend up to two hours visualizing and anticipating. Man advantage, 5-on-4, right-handed shot, this is what I'm gonna do. That was my preparation. I did not care about how other goalies looked. I was going to play my game and use my system. That's the way I lived my life.

I have never been unsure in my whole life. The confidence was always there, but as soon as I worked with Plante, that's when the magic happened.

We finished fourth my first year in Toronto. When it came time to negotiate a new contract, my agent, Howard Casper, and I ran into problems. Howard could be crude and rude.

I was in the middle year of the deal I'd signed with Philadelphia. During the summer Toronto offered a new three-year deal that fell short of what we expected.

They raised their offer to $30,000, then $35,000, and then $40,000, but Casper said that wasn't enough. We got up and walked out of the meeting. We talked once more and got to within $2,000 apart, but we never closed the gap.

The taxes were brutal in Canada, and we talked about incorporating me in the United States, but they squelched that idea. I never signed a contract, and that's why I was free to go to the World Hockey Association when they came calling.

I have always taken risks in my life. That's one of the reasons I wrote a book called *Risk and Fear*. Here I was, playing for Toronto, a well-established team in a well-established league. And then I got a telephone call from someone in the World Hockey Association, asking if I'd like to join them.

It was a calculated risk on my part. They were offering me a lot more money than I was making in Toronto—four times as much. I went to Howard Ballard, owner of the Maple Leafs, and told him I would stay in Toronto if I got another $5,000 per year. Ballard tossed me out of his office. He said the new league would never make it. He said I was a loser. Well, as it turned out, Ballard lost nine players to the new league. *Nine* players, and the Leafs never recovered from that.

I flew to Miami and signed a contract to play for the Screaming Eagles. They posed me with a jersey. I still have that jersey. It might be the only one they made, so it's probably worth a lot of money. They put us up in a $100-a-day suite in a fancy hotel. I was 27, sitting in Miami, a warm place, and enjoying the excitement of a new team in a new league. So what if the only ice they had was in a highball glass? My philosophy has always been to be optimistic. Why think about negatives? Hey, if it doesn't work out, learn from it and move on.

When I got on that plane to Miami with Carol, I saw John McLellan, my coach in Toronto. What were the odds? He had a problem with stomach ulcers and was going to Miami to see a specialist and to unwind a little. He saw me and asked, "What are you doing on this flight?" I told him I was going to Miami to sign with the WHA.

I could tell, *boom*, his ulcers started acting up, and he started swallowing medicine.

I signed with Miami at 2:00 in the afternoon. By the time I got home that night, they had become the Philadelphia Blazers. The whole picture changed while we were on that plane.

The deal was for five years for something like $750,000, plus the extras, including a new car every season. I didn't think of myself as a pioneer, but in a sense I guess I was. I was a little like Joe Namath; when he signed with the Jets in the AFL, he changed the salary structure in the old league. And that's what happened after I signed.

We wound up playing in front of 500 or 600 people. I was accustomed to playing in front of 18,000. You miss the fans. The crowd, especially in your home rink, can lift you to a

PHILADELPHIA BLAZERS HOCKEY CLUB

WORLD HOCKEY ASSOCIATION

OFFICIAL PROGRAM AND MAGAZINE $1.00

WELCOME HOME

Crusaders Cleveland

New England Whalers

Raiders

Houston Aeros

Andre Lacroix Bernie Parent

Alberta Oilers Edmonton

Chicago Cougars

Ottawa Nationals

Los Angeles Sharks

Nordiques Quebec

Winnipeg Jets Hockey Club

Minnesota Fighting Saints

Vol. I No. 1

SHER-WOOD
00

higher level. It's like being a singer on stage in front of a huge audience; it brings out the best in the performer.

In the beginning, Jim Cooper, an attorney and a real nice guy, was a big part of the Blazers. I remember he had this idea of eliminating tie games. He wanted the teams to play a five-minute overtime, and if the game was still tied, have a shootout.

I hated that idea, but it was still better than Stu Nahan's idea. Stu was a popular television guy in Philadelphia. He did a kid's show for a while, where he played Captain Philadelphia, before he became a hockey announcer. Stu thought it would improve the game if we used a *white* puck. He must have hated goalies. Later on, he showed up in all the *Rocky* movies as the fight announcer. I think Sylvester Stallone thought of him as a good-luck charm.

Cooper was smart and he cared about the players. But, eventually, he stopped being involved, and a trucking company guy named Bernie Brown started running things.

They wanted me to wear No. 00 on my jersey, as in the number of goals I was going to allow. I thought that when somebody scored, I would turn around and people would holler, "Oh, Oh!"

So, how did I deal with the pressure of a home opener, on a new team, in a new league? I went hunting, that's how.

It was the last day of the season for using a bow and arrow. So that's what I used. I went out into the woods near the ATCO Raceway. That was my way to relax, a natural way to get my mind clear. Better than going to a movie, or out to dinner. Got a deer.

The city of Philadelphia wanted us to play in town. They spent a lot of money fixing up Convention Hall, but opening night was a disaster. The ice broke up, and the fans threw souvenir pucks onto the rink. Derek Sanderson, our star player, got hurt, and I broke a bone in my foot stopping a shot.

Soon rumors started swirling that the franchise was being moved, maybe even as far away as Vancouver. The checks stopped coming. My agent warned them that if they didn't pay on time, I wouldn't play. To me, that made sense. You know it's not going to be a popular decision, but you have to do what's right. You have to stand up for what you believe.

My time in the WHA was part of the journey, part of the learning process. I had no idea at the time that I would be back with the Flyers, but I did have confidence that I could play in the NHL. I had put to work what I had learned from Plante. Sure, I was facing 50 shots a game with the Blazers, because that's the way they played in the WHA. When I walked away, one columnist wrote that I deserved equal amounts of pity and scorn. The coach, John McKenzie, ripped me. I know some of the players were unhappy with me.

When you believe in yourself and in your purpose in life, you don't pay attention to what people think. Society tells you to fit in. Whatever the cost, you're supposed to fit in. But what if it means giving up your freedom? What if it interrupts your march toward your purpose? I refuse to go that route. If no one is harmed by your actions, you do what you feel is right. It doesn't matter what people think.

I consider myself a wolf, as opposed to a dog. The dog lives in a warm home, is fed all the time, and sleeps in the same bed as his owners. He has a beautiful life. There comes a time when he has to go outside, fenced in or on a leash. He loses his freedom.

Look at the wolf. Sure, he can be ragged looking at times, and he has to endure cold winters, rain and sleet, and the heat of summer. But he has one thing the dog does not have, and that's his freedom.

I never understood that principle until I got older. It explains how I reacted throughout my entire life. I'm not someone who can organize things or plan for the future. I'm spontaneous. If something doesn't work, I learn from it and move on. It doesn't matter what your wife thinks, your kids think, or your friends think. What matters is what *you* think. Until you come to grips with that, you're simply a people pleaser. And that's not my personality. I'm not here to live someone else's dreams; I'm here to live *my* dreams.

Some people would say that is selfish. But I don't think doing what you want is selfish; being selfish is having other people do the things you want.

"RIGHT DOWN SHERO'S ALLEY"

Fred Shero had a chronically bad back, so he could not sit still for long periods of time. He had a phantom presence, stopping in a bar long enough for a beer, a cigarette, and then poof, he was gone. Somewhere in his wandering that night in Atlanta he got mugged and had to miss a playoff game. (Originally published in the Philadelphia Daily News, *April 15, 1974)*

ATLANTA—Fred Shero walks a lot. Alone. At all hours of the night. In cruddy neighborhoods. Drifting in and out of crumby places. A beer, two cigarettes, and on his way again.

"He'll get up at three in the morning and walk," said assistant coach Mike Nykoluk last night.

"If you're due in at 11 and it's one in the morning, and you walk down some dark alley, Freddie is the guy you're gonna run into," said Flyers captain Bobby Clarke.

"He walks alone, always deep in thought," said general manager Keith Allen.

"Freddie is Freddie," said team owner Ed Snider. "We saw him before the team meeting Saturday night. Walking. We said, 'Hey, Freddie, don't walk too far…we hear these streets aren't safe.'"

Nobody could tell Fred Shero about urban blight and high crime rate and unsafe streets. He kept walking those desolate alleyways, drifting in and out of musty places, unaware, unafraid.

"They call him 'Phantom'", Clarke said last night after the Flyers rallied to beat Atlanta 4–3 in overtime and complete a four-game sweep of their playoff series.

"He'd go into some of the dingiest places you ever saw, have a cigarette and a beer, and leave. He liked to keep walking because he has a bad back."

Some therapy. Saturday night, after the team meeting, somewhere, sometime, somehow, Fred Shero got beat up. Shero says he cannot remember how it happened, how his glasses got shattered, his arm got slashed, his thumb busted.

Who knows? It might have happened in his hotel room because that's where Nykoluk found him dazed and bloodied Sunday morning.

He was too groggy to coach the team last night, so he headed home and Nykoluk stepped in. First, the beefy assistant had to tell the team. He told them in the locker room at the Omni before the pregame warmup.

"We thought about making excuses," Nykoluk said. "Then, we figured Fred has been so honest with them all year, we'd tell them the truth, what we knew.

"It was nothing to be ashamed about…it was regrettable, that's all. I told them we owed something to the guy who should be behind the bench."

"We didn't find out until just before we went out on the ice," Clarke said. "I don't know how anybody felt about it. Mike said we owed the man something and it's obvious we do. But he didn't say we owe Freddie a win."

This was a Stanley Cup playoff game. Nykoluk knew he didn't need to send the players crashing wild-eyed through glass partitions at the thought of winning one for Fred Shero.

Whatever emotions were churning inside those orange uniforms, the Flyers fell behind 3–0. "We played loose the first period," Clarke said clinically. "The only period in the playoffs we played loose."

But before the "Gipper" could turn over in his grave, Dave Schultz got into a fistfight with Bryan Hextall, beating Hextall's face to a pulp with the wrong hand, his left.

"Ahhhh," Schultz said afterward, "I thought about switching hands, but I was holding his jersey with the right hand. And the right hand is banged up anyway."

Before Hextall's forehead stopped bleeding, the Flyers scored a goal. They got two more in the third period to send the game screeching into overtime. That made the fistfight the turning point on those imaginary box scores people like to keep.

"Ahhhh, I don't know about that," said Schultz humbly.

"I don't know if a fight turns a game around," said Terry Crisp. "But it lets you know you're still in the game even though you're down three goals. Guys are still interested in winning.

"You see Dave is in there swinging. And later on, other guys get to swinging, when we're down two goals. So everybody says, 'Why can't we do it?'"

So they did it. Goals by Gary Dornhoefer after being belted twice, and by Tom Baldon, who kept cranking out shots all night, and it was a tie game.

"We should have won it in the third period," Nykoluk squeaked afterward, that small voice coming out of that large chest, like getting sarsaparilla out of a beer keg.

Chalk up one for emotion? Or one for a punch in the snoot? How about chalking up this one to strategy and skill, those weary old intangibles?

Shero suggested to Nykoluk that he wanted Schultz out there with Clarke and Bill Flett because he wanted Bill Barber's speed matched against Tom Lysiak's line. So Schultz was out there in the tense overtime, on Clarke's line.

And there they were 2-on-1, in the overtime. And after Clarke lured the lone defenseman into his shadow, he slipped a perfect pass to the lonesome Schultz.

"Ordinarily," Schultz said in that raspy honest way he has, "I'd shoot it into his pads. This time, instead of winding up, I just stuffed it in."

He stuffed it past Phil Myre and the game was over and a fan conked him with an air horn, but he hardly blinked, he was so happy.

"You know what this proves," deep thinker Bernie Parent announced on the giddy flight home. "This proves we've got a helluva team."

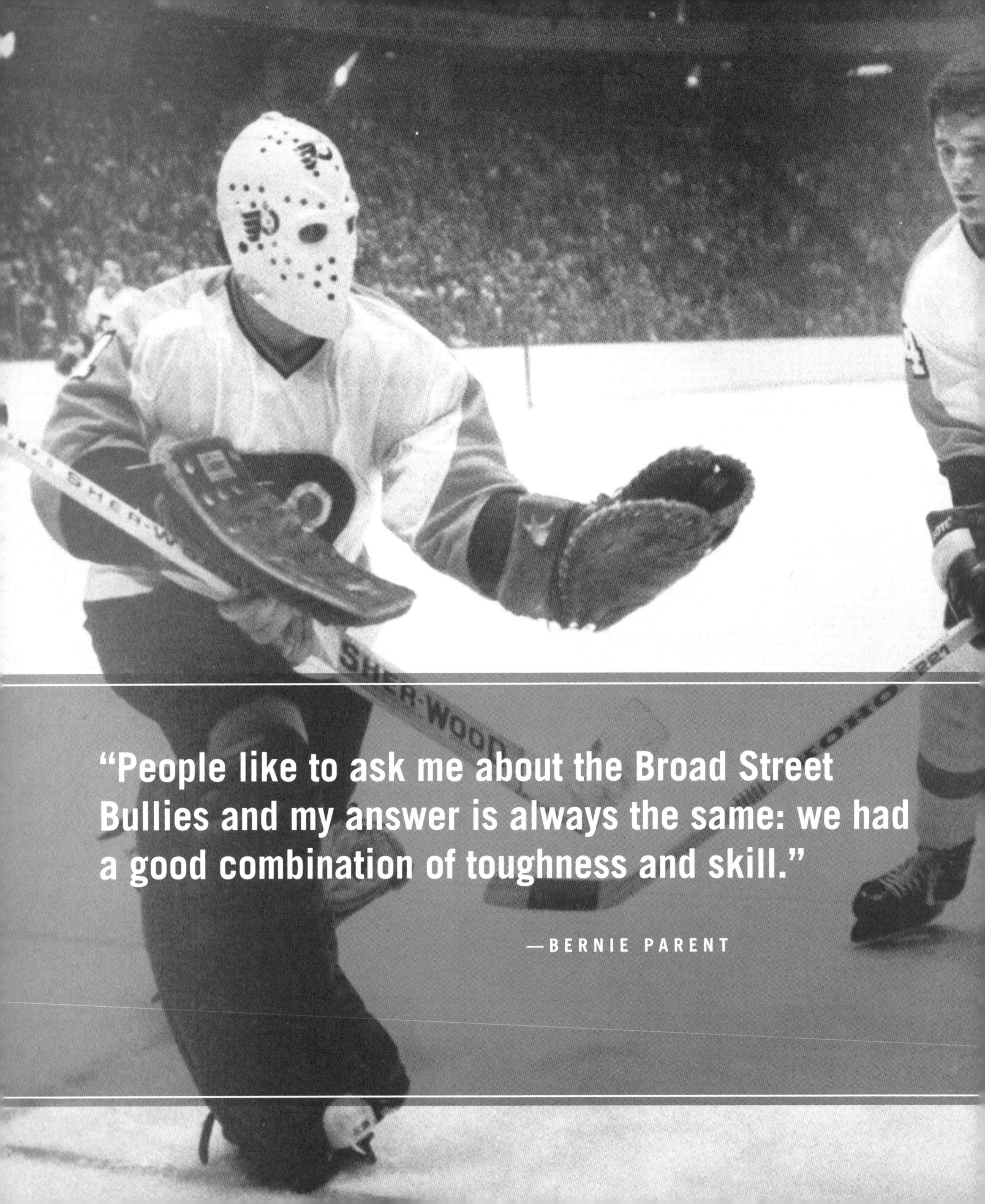

“People like to ask me about the Broad Street Bullies and my answer is always the same: we had a good combination of toughness and skill.”

—BERNIE PARENT

CHAPTER FOUR

HOCKEY HEAVEN

I was surprised that the Flyers wanted me back. I knew what I could do as a goalie, but Doug Favell was playing well for them. The year before, I remember going to a playoff game at the Spectrum where the Flyers were playing Montreal in the semifinals. I sat upstairs with a friend. It was weird to be there as a spectator. Favell had a good game.

I got the news that the Flyers made a deal with Toronto to bring me back while I was on a cruise to Martinique. I celebrated the whole day. I celebrated the next five days, too. I do not remember much about Martinique. Eventually I stopped celebrating and thought about how popular Favell was with the fans. I didn't know how I'd be received. Lots of question marks. Would I fit in? If not, I'd have to work at it.

I look back and I'm still amazed at what happened that year. Seven years earlier, when the Flyers were introduced to Philadelphia, they paraded us down Broad Street through the center of town. Ten people showed up, plus a great dane and a poodle. It might have been nine people, with another guy just wandering through, looking for work.

Seven years later we win the Stanley Cup and 2 million people show up for the parade. It was overwhelming.

But that's getting ahead of the story. We played a tough season, and battled our way through the playoffs against long odds. We were the Broad Street Bullies, loved at home and hated on the road and probably in the league offices.

We had a mysterious coach. And we had each other.

After the Flyers got manhandled by St. Louis in the playoffs, Mr. Snider vowed that would never happen again, which is how we became the Broad Street Bullies. Mr. Snider told *The New York Times* that we would never again get pushed around. We might not be able to outskate everybody, but we could get guys that could fight as well as anybody else.

In the old days, he said, prior to the Blues terrorizing us, teams had what they called a policeman, guys like John Ferguson in Montreal. Mr. Snider asked his hockey people if there was any rule saying that you couldn't have more than one. We sort of changed the philosophy at the time.

It's important to remember that even though we led the league in penalty minutes for 11 straight years, we also had some talented players on our team.

Bobby Clarke was our captain, the youngest captain in the National Hockey League. He was the greatest leader I've ever played with. He was a very caring person. Combine those two qualities, leadership and caring, and you have a super individual.

It started with his work habits, which were just incredible. They elevated the entire team. He set the tone for the way we practiced, the way we played. I'm sure a lot of his work ethic came from growing up in the mining town of Flin Flon. Orest Kindrachuk once told Clarke that Flin Flon is just five miles north of where civilization ends.

He was a diabetic, which is how the Flyers were able to get him deep in the draft. But that didn't affect the way he played, and it didn't affect the way we thought about him.

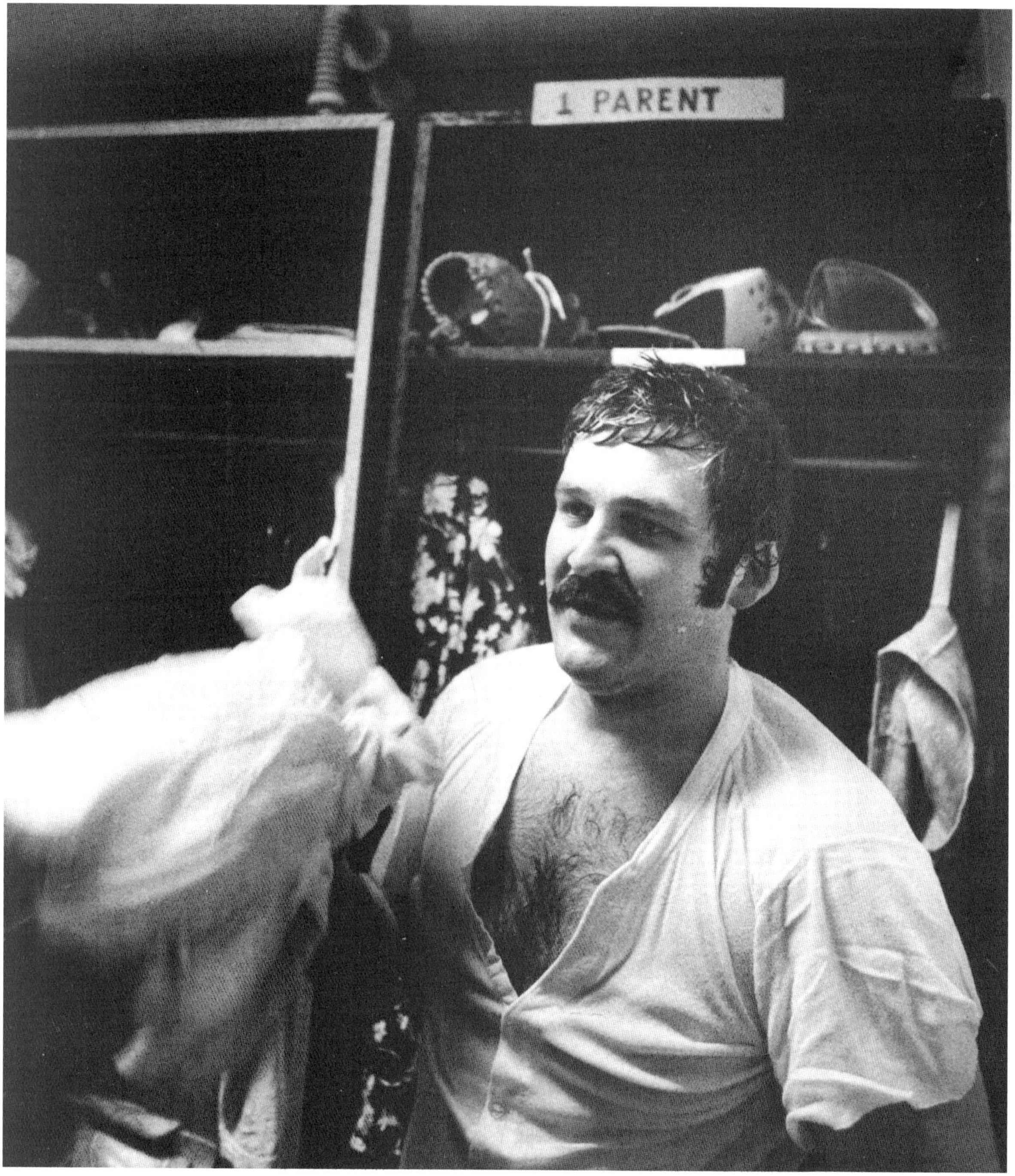
1 PARENT

If somebody had problems, Clarke was always there to help.

He never yelled in the room. He said things calmly and quietly. Mostly, he talked to guys one on one if he felt they weren't performing at the level he thought they should. He would not embarrass anyone by pointing a finger.

Clarke could defend himself in a fight, and there was nothing cowardly about him. If someone cheap-shotted him and his teammates stepped in, it was to make sure he didn't get hurt, because his leadership was so important to the team.

Clarke would always tell people that the Flyers had pretty much the same image and philosophy from the time they started. He said we were always an entertaining, tough team with a personality. He would say, if you're not easy to hate, then what are you?

We had Rick MacLeish, who everyone called "Cutey." That was because his nose went sideways. Nicknames don't have to make sense. He was a very, very quiet individual. He had great skating and hockey skills and a terrific wrist shot. He was an amazing skater, too. Clarke could skate for a whole month, two hours a day. Rick could skate two or three times a month and still outskate Clarke in a game. It just seemed so natural for him.

Because Rick made it look easy, he got criticized sometimes. Guys took turns trying to get him up for games. The thing is, he got better as the season went on, and he seemed to be at his best in the playoffs.

The next year, Clarke talked about MacLeish. He said, "He's got fewer goals this year, but he contributed more. We won more. Sometimes a good game doesn't look that way because he has so much natural ability. An off night for him is maybe a good night for another guy."

We had Gary Dornhoefer, who we called "The 20-Million Dollar Man" because he wound up with new hips, new knees, and a repaired shoulder. He was a much-better-than-average right winger. Not Guy Lafleur, but very good. He had no fear, and showed that by standing in front of the net, taking punishment, which is why he wound up with 10 different replacement parts. He wasn't afraid to pay the price to score a goal.

Gary once tried to explain why he was willing to take that beating. "I've got to do my thing," he said. "I can't skate, I can't shoot, I can't see too good, and I can't fight too good."

Bill Barber is another one of those guys who got overshadowed. I compare him to Joe Frazier, who was a terrific heavyweight champion. But Frazier came along at the same time as Muhammad Ali, and because Ali had so much more charisma, people loved him and overlooked Frazier.

Barber was the same way. I think he was one of the best left wingers in the history of the game. Strong, solid, good skater, good shot. He's in the Hall of Fame, for goodness sake. But it wasn't until he got put on the same line with Clarke and Reggie Leach that people paid attention to him. That was an incredible line; those guys knew where the other guys would be, and Barber and Leach fed off Clarke's skills with the puck.

We also had Eddie Van Impe. Steady Eddie was very smart, with average talent. He used his intelligence to put himself in the right place at the right time. He could anticipate what was going to happen next. Plus, he was feared because of what he could do with his stick. In the old days, if you speared somebody, you got a standing ovation. It's different now, but back in the day, he planted fear in other guys.

The thing I remember most about Terry Crisp is his smile. He was a grinder, like a lot of players on our team. You need that combination of skilled players and grinders. The grinders do their work along the boards, fighting to control the puck. Relentless guys. Crisp was like that. It compensated for his soft shot. I remember he scored on me in practice one day and I wanted to retire on the spot. I remember how Doug Favell used to taunt Crispy in practice. He'd drop his glove on the ice and catch Crisp's shot barehanded.

One guy I was really fond of was Bobby Taylor, the backup goalie after Favell got traded. Backup goaltender is a very tough job. I liked playing a lot of games. When you're not playing, you're not getting any younger. I knew Bobby could play well if he got the chance. But if you play two games a season, how can you improve? My first eight or nine years in the NHL, I'd only miss maybe four games with injuries.

I never had to be in that position, just sitting around. I knew it was awful. I remember one game, the fans had a banner that said, "Chucky Margolis says Bobby Taylor will razzle-dazzle

his opponents." Afterward, Bobby told me what it was all about. I guess it was a kids' program on Saturday mornings on Channel 10. He'd get home from practice, flip it on, and laugh his head off, the same way I loved to watch The Three Stooges. He didn't play for months and then he got the chance against Pittsburgh, and Fred Shero yanked him after two periods.

Bobby said he tried to keep his hockey life separate from his personal life, but that his wife took an awful brow-beating. He said that lots of times, he couldn't fall asleep until 5:00 in the morning wondering what was becoming of his career.

Outwardly, he seemed to handle his situation well. He said that every guy who gets to the NHL gets there because he's a tough competitor. He said you have to have pride in yourself, you have to want to play. Then he said that the only consolation was that he was the backup goalie to the best goaltender in the world, and that made me feel good.

Moose, aka Andre Dupont, was a big ball of energy. Strong. He had a winning attitude, and he brought his enthusiasm onto the ice with him.

Some people questioned the Moose Shuffle, the little dance he did when he scored a goal. But that was who he was.

He wasn't taunting anyone, he wasn't dancing in anyone's face, it was just a small celebration of what he had accomplished.

Our general manager was Keith Allen. I had met him in 1967 when he was the coach of the Flyers. We had a game one night in Chicago. We lost 12–0. They had Bobby Hull and Stan Mikita. Favell had started and gave up six goals. Keith came up behind me and said, "You're going in." I said, "Are you crazy?" Hull was firing the puck 120 miles an hour and they had a team full of great players. He almost yanked me up by my armpits and shoved me out there.

Then came the disaster against St. Louis, when they hammered us on the ice and on the scoreboard. When Allen became the general manager, he made the decision along with Mr. Snider that the team had to get bigger, stronger, and tougher.

Mr. Snider has always done it that way; he gives people the chance to do what they're supposed to do. And if it doesn't work, he brings in different people. He gave Keith the green light to change things, and Keith did a fantastic job. Sometimes new players don't fit in. But Keith brought in guys who did fit in. He was a master at reading players. They nicknamed him Keith the Thief because we always seemed to end up with the better side of every trade.

When we were celebrating our first Stanley Cup, he was in the locker room talking to Bobby Clarke and Bobby's father, asking about Reggie Leach and how they thought he'd fit in. And then he went out and got him. A lot of people didn't agree with bringing me back from Toronto, after the World Hockey experience. But Keith stuck his neck out and brought me back, and I'll never forget that.

When the season started, I was ready. We played Toronto, with Favell in their goal, and we won 2–0. Afterward, Freddie Shero said I was the greatest goalie he'd ever coached. After one game!

It was the first of 12 shutouts that year and people made a big fuss about that, but that statistic wasn't high on my list. It wasn't like I was standing on my head to get those shutouts. Defensively, Freddie had the guys playing really well in front of me. The other team didn't have a lot of great opportunities.

In the World Hockey League you thought about surviving, not shutouts. To me, 12 shutouts was no big deal. The focus was more on winning. I'd rather win a game 15–14 than lose it 1–0. If we won a game with a shutout, so be it. It was cool, sure. But it wasn't like we were obsessed with collecting shutouts. The win was satisfying enough.

A shutout is like a perfect game—everything has to go right.

The defensemen have to clear guys out of my crease so I can see the shots coming. We don't give up any odd-man breaks. Everybody does his job.

When I look back at that season, we won 51 games, we finished first in the West Division, and we won the Stanley Cup. Shutouts would be at the bottom of the list of what we accomplished. As a kid, my goal was to someday win the Stanley Cup—that was the top priority. Along the way, there's the challenge of winning certain awards, and the Vezina was one of them. Look at the list of guys who have won it—that's a special group of goalies. And then realize that you have to be on the right team to have a chance to accomplish those things. So that year, and the next one, provided tremendous memories for me.

People like to ask me about the Broad Street Bullies and my answer is always the same: we had a good combination of toughness and skill.

They made a documentary about that team, and Phil Esposito said that you don't win a championship just on toughness, that you have to have skills. We had a lot of players with skills. It was a tremendous team and we shared a strong bond. We killed penalties well. It wasn't just a one-man deal; it wasn't just about the goalie. We led the league in penalty minutes, but the toughness we had compensated for being a man short.

Plus, we had a loud, loyal crowd on our side. I think 75 percent of our success was due to the crowd. I was recently digging around in a closet and I found a ticket stub for the Finals that year. The ticket cost $9.50. We were getting families coming to our games. During warmups, you could hear them greet each other: "How's Jimmy doing?" or "I hear your daughter got married." They knew each other. It was like one big family.

At some point, Lou Scheinfeld put on a recording of Kate Smith singing "God Bless America," and it caught on. Fans sang along. She became a good-luck charm. It got to be a ritual. Kate would sing, and we would win. Then she started showing up in person. The cynical people—mainly sportswriters—would ask how a heavy-set American woman on the downward side of her career could inspire a bunch of Canadians by singing "God Bless America."

I knew there was magic to her. The universe that provides life with trees, oceans, and people is the same universe that provides life for Americans, Canadians, and Egyptians. You had this lady singing "God Bless America" and the magic was there. It didn't matter where you were born, where you grew up, or where you lived.

It built up throughout the year. I think we were 38–3–1 when she sang. Psychologically, it

16
5

gave us an edge. When she showed up in the Finals, Esposito tried to cancel the hex and gave her a bouquet of flowers. She handed them to her organist and gave Espo the finger. We knew then she wasn't just making an appearance—she really wanted us to win.

We clinched the division championship by beating Boston 5–3, the first time we'd beaten the Bruins in five years. They dropped orange and black balloons from the rafters after the game. Afterward, Freddie Shero said we hadn't won anything yet, that it was only a step.

Freddie saved some of his best quotations for the playoffs. I remember during the season he once wrote on the blackboard, "An oak tree is just a nut that held its ground."

Barry Ashbee wrote underneath it, "If you can walk with your head in the clouds and keep your feet on the ground, you can make a million dollars in the National Basketball Association."

Some coaches in the league scattered money around the room before the playoffs started to remind players what was at stake. Freddie scoffed at that trick. He said, "You've got to appeal to them in different ways...prestige and pride. Your record lives forever. The money's not gonna last forever."

The playoffs are different from the regular season in so many ways. There are fewer flights, fewer penalties, and fewer odd-man rushes. The fans are different. The noise in the building is different, too. There's some fear mixed in there. Back in the day, that first round of the playoffs was best of five. A team could wind up being out of it in a hurry if it lost a game at home.

Freddie was a master at getting us ready, stressing that we had to be prepared, and that we had to keep doing the things that got us there in the first place.

We faced Atlanta in the opening round of the playoffs. We beat them 4–1 in the first game with Orest Kindrachuk scoring two goals. The second game we beat them 5–1 with Rick MacLeish scoring a hat trick. Then we went to Atlanta and beat them 4–1 in a crazy game that included a brawl when both benches emptied. There was a dispute over a MacLeish goal past Dan Bouchard with the referee, Dave Newell, overruling the goal judge who didn't light the lamp.

We were up 3–0 in the series and that's when Freddie Shero got mugged. We still don't know what happened, but he did have a habit of wandering the streets. Some guys called him "Phantom" because he never stayed in one place too long.

They didn't tell us about Freddie until just before the pregame warmup. Mike Nykoluk coached the game and we fell behind 3–0 in the first period. And then Dave Schultz got into a fight with Bryan Hextall and pounded his face until it was bloody.

I'm not saying that turned the game around, but we rallied and tied it up 3–3. And then Nykoluk put Schultz out there in overtime and he took a pass from Clarke and stuffed the puck past Phil Myre and the series was over.

I told people afterward, "You know what this proves? It proves we've got a helluva team."

The Rangers were up next. The writers couldn't wait to remind us that we were 1–12–6 over the past seven seasons in Madison Square

Garden. Some of us reminded the writers that the Rangers hadn't won a Stanley Cup since 1940.

Dave Schultz took it one step too far. Before the first game, Schultz said he was happy to face a team with a reputation for choking. Those 1974 semifinals was the first time we played the Rangers in the playoffs. Now, it seems like a regular thing. We've met 10 times in the playoffs and won six times. And if you're wondering, familiarity does breed contempt.

At the time, I felt that the most important thing was to focus on your objectives. I feel the same way today. You do that, and the negatives fall apart. They disappear. We had home-ice advantage against the Rangers. We felt good about that. As it turned out, we lost all three in New York, but we won all four in Philadelphia.

We zapped them 4–0 in the first game in Philly. I only had to face seven shots in the first two periods, which tells you what kind of job the defense was doing.

I made sure I praised the Rangers afterward. I said that they were a great machine and that you had to respect them. We got a shutout because we followed our system, and when we did that we didn't make a lot of mistakes in our own end. We didn't give away the puck.

We thumped them 5–2 in the second game. Their goalie, Ed Giacomin, banged his stick against the glass in front of the goal judge after Eddie Van Impe scored on a backhanded shot.

The series moved to Madison Square Garden and we squandered a 3–1 lead and lost 5–3. We got called for 81 minutes in penalties, so the Rangers wound up with 11 power plays. Freddie got confused when he said he thought Pearl Harbor was over in 1942, missing it by a year, but most of us were just as angry at the way the game was called. Clarence Campbell, the league president, was angry, too. He said it injured the league's image.

The Rangers tied up the series in Game 4, winning 2–1 in overtime. We scored first on a Joe Watson goal, but then they gave Bobby Rousseau a goal on a shot that hit my glove. I never saw it cross the line but the goal judge thought it did.

Rod Gilbert deflected in the winning goal in overtime, less than a minute after we lost Barry Ashbee. Dale Rolfe got off a shot and the puck hit Ashbee in the eye, ending his career.

Ashbee was such a good, strong defenseman. I could hear the puck hit him in the face. When he went down, we knew it was serious.

We'd already lost Bob Kelly, and now Ashbee was out. That's when Clarke stepped forward; that's when his leadership made the difference. People had a certain image of the Broad Street Bullies. But we were about to demonstrate a different image.

We were known for being tough on the ice, but now we had to show a mental toughness. We knew we had to move on. We had a chance to win one for our buddy. We had to keep our focus, win the next game, win the series, and move on. And that's what we did.

Back at the Spectrum, we won the fifth game 4–1. Bingo—they came right back at us in Game 6 at the Garden, winning by the same score.

Before Game 7, Gump Worsley was quoted as saying, "Bernie is playing like Jacques Plante in his heyday, but there is no way a man can keep going like he is going. Not even Plante could do that."

When it was over, Worsley had more kind words for me. "The thing that amazes me," he said, "is the way he handles the pressure.

SHERWOOD

Physically doing the job, that's one thing. But playing in goal, that's as much a mental thing as well. I've been there, I know the feeling. Bernie Parent handles the pressure as well as anyone I've seen."

Freddie had checked us into a motel in Valley Forge, Pennsylvania. I woke up at 7:00 in the morning, thinking that it was going to be the biggest game I ever played in. It was still scoreless in the first period when Schultz hammered Dale Rolfe after a shoving match. Schultz yanked his hair, hit him with 17 straight shots, and bloodied his face. Nobody on that Rangers team came to his defense. Some people think that set the tone for the game, and we won it 4–3 to advance to the Stanley Cup Finals against Boston.

Afterward, Emile Francis, the Rangers coach and general manager, grumbled that he had too many "fat cats" on his team. For years, the Rangers were remembered bitterly for standing around and watching Rolfe get beat up.

Finally, just before the Winter Carnival alumni game, Brad Park told the *New York Post*, "Let's get something straight…we did not meekly stand by…we were forced to stand by. It was Game 7, the league had brought the third-man-in rule, so somebody would have gotten thrown out of the game with a game misconduct.

"So who did you want to lose: Rod Gilbert, Jean Ratelle, Vic Hadfield, or myself? I did decide to go, but Dale looked me in the eye and said to stay out of it."

Freddie Shero said at the time that the fight took something out of New York. Park said he was nearly sickened by our tactics. He said, "I decided if I had to maim somebody to win the Stanley Cup, it wasn't worth it. It's a sport. It's entertainment, right?"

Park's mother was asked if she would invite any of the Flyers to dinner. She said, "I wouldn't invite them to my garage."

They told me later that the series against the Rangers set a record for penalty minutes. What I do remember about the final game was being caught up in the moment, in the excitement. I walked back into the locker room and remembered being a kid and wondering what it would be like to be in the Finals. Now we had beaten the Rangers and I didn't have to wonder anymore. I was there. It was overwhelming, this realization that we were in the Finals.

That's why we beat Boston, in the end. Instead of worrying about playing afraid, we were dancing in a dream. It didn't matter who we were playing against; there were no limitations on us. It was a beautiful approach and we took it.

You're in the Finals, something you dreamed about as a kid, and it's like an out-of-body experience. You're floating. What a wonderful feeling. You picture the Stanley Cup. It's in your mind 24/7. You fantasize about skating around the rink holding the Cup over your head. You think you're riding in a cloud in a blue sky, holding the Cup.

Once the games start, however, it's a war and not even close to those dreams. Once the war is over, you allow yourself to dream again and that's when the magic happens. The actual physical part, the games, that's war.

Before the Finals, the writers couldn't wait to remind us that we were 0–16–2 in Boston since our first visit in 1967. The Bruins had beaten Chicago in six games in their semifinals, so they were coming off a week's rest.

We finished that brutal seven-game series with the Rangers on a Sunday. Monday we arrived in Boston and there was a story that quoted Freddie Shero as saying the Finals would be anticlimactic because we had just beaten the best team in hockey.

Joe Watson screamed at Shero about that one. Freddie just pushed the glasses back on his nose and said, "We haven't beaten them in seven years, let's give 'em something to think about."

We were 0–17–2 after Boston beat us 3–2 in the opener. We had played well, especially defensively. We were not discouraged. Then we ended the famine by beating them 3–2 in overtime in Game 2 with Clarke scoring the winning goal off an assist by Dave Schultz.

Schultz? On a line with Clarke and Cowboy Flett? In overtime? Freddie pushed his glasses back on the bridge of his nose and told people, "For a while, we were going with our best shooters. All of a sudden I realized Schultz has no business sitting on the bench, not after what he contributed to us all year."

1
PARENT

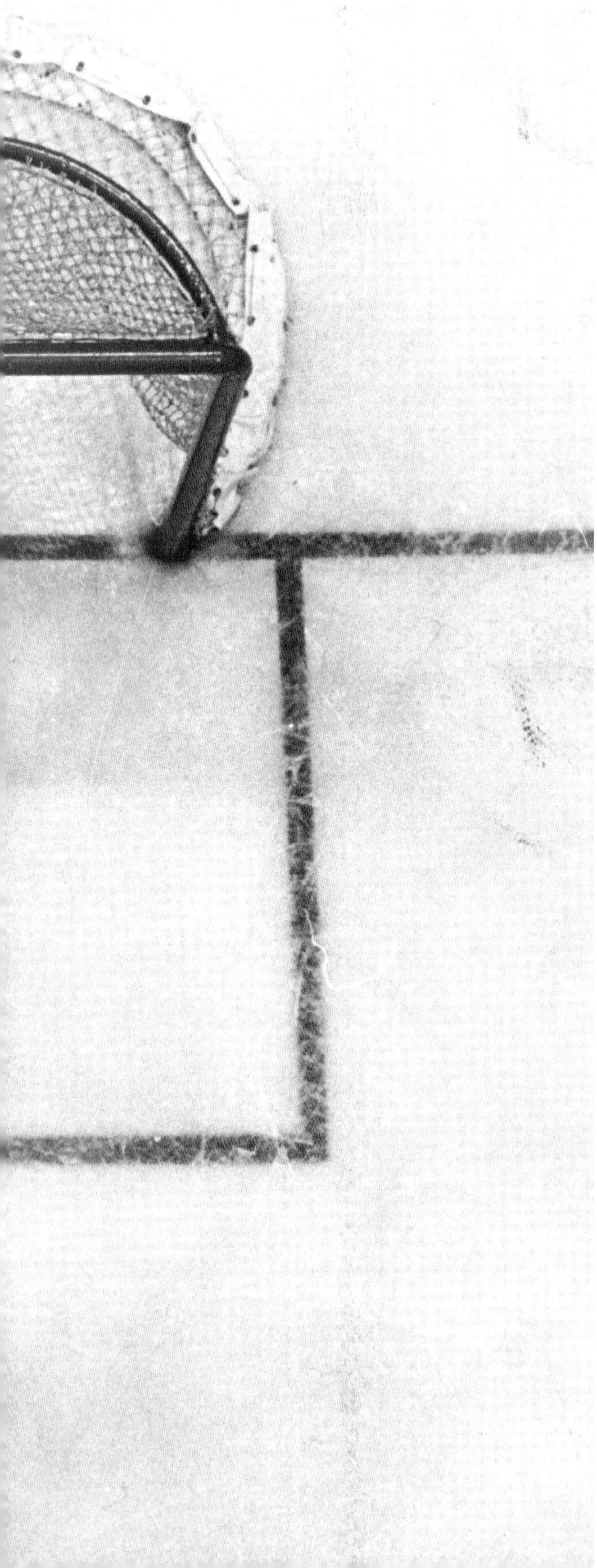

Schultz dug the puck out of a corner and threw a blind pass to Clarke, who tried to backhand it past Gil Gilbert. Gilbert batted it away but Clarke lifted the rebound over Gilbert and into the net.

We took the lead in the series with a 4–1 win back at the Spectrum, and the grinders were the heroes that night. Guys like Tom Bladon, Terry Crisp, and Orest Kindrachuk. Freddie reminded people that guys like Tom Bladon, Terry Crisp, and Orest Kindrachuk had helped us win all year. Freddie's approach to using his bench was, use it or lose it. We fell behind 1–0, tied it up, and then Crisp scored with a typical soft shot past Gilbert.

Afterward Crisp talked about the needling he got about his shot and mentioned Bobby Taylor teasing him in practice, taking off his mask and saying he was going to catch the next one in his teeth. He also talked about what he'd learned from Hap Emms: when you win, say little. And when you lose, say less.

Meanwhile, the casualty list got longer. We'd lost Ashbee to that terrible eye injury. We lost Bob Kelly. And then we lost Dornhoefer with a separated left shoulder that needed surgery. But other guys stepped up. In Game 4, Ed Van Impe played the game of his life and we won 4–2. Eddie had waited 14 years for the chance to drink from the Cup, and now we were one win away.

Somebody asked me why I always kept my mask on. Partly because of nerves, I told him. Partly because of habit. But if we won the Cup in Boston, I guaranteed I'd take that thing off after the final horn.

I didn't get to keep that promise, because the Bruins won the fifth game 5–1. We got whistled for 24 penalties and couldn't get anything going.

We had brought some champagne with us to Boston, and we had to lug it back to Philadelphia. I'm not superstitious, so I didn't think that had anything to do with the way we played that day.

The loss set up the drama of Game 6, at home, and we were ready. Barry Ashbee showed up and sat in the owner's box, and he got a standing ovation when they showed him on the big video screen.

Rick MacLeish defelected in a slap shot by Moose Dupont late in the first period, and that was all the scoring. With about three minutes to go, the Bruins had their last good chance to tie it. Ken Hodge, a right-handed shot, came down on my left side and got off a slap shot from about 30 feet out, but I deflected it with my stick.

With 2:22 left, Bobby Orr dragged down Bobby Clarke and got two minutes for holding. Bep Guidolin, the Boston coach, squawked about the call, but it looked good to me. I remember thinking, *Thank you, Lord.*

With 40 seconds left in the game, there was a faceoff in our end. In those days, you could stop the action before the ref dropped the puck.

I yelled, "Hold on!" I called Joe Watson over. Everyone thought we were talking about how we were gonna play the faceoff.

"I said to him, 'We win tonight, the women are gonna be lined up outside our door all summer long.'" He screamed at me, asking what was wrong with me. I just thought it was a good way to take some of the pressure off.

There was one final, scary moment. I told Mr. Snider about it a few years ago and he almost had a heart attack. There were eight seconds left in the game and a faceoff in Boston's end. Think about it—everybody's standing, everybody's screaming loud enough to raise the roof. I still get goose bumps thinking about it.

We were leading 1–0, and if we could hold on, we'd win the Stanley Cup. Boston won the faceoff, Orr got the puck, and he shot it down the ice. I was looking at the clock, watching the seconds tick off. *Pow!* The puck missed the net and hit the boards behind me.

Joe Watson went back there and touched it, but the referee let those last three seconds tick away.

Gene Hart was screaming on the radio, "The Flyers win the Cup! The Flyers win the Cup! The Flyers have won the Stanley Cup!" It was a great call.

They brought the Cup out and handed it to Bobby Clarke. He turned to me, and said, "Benny [he always called me Benny], grab hold of the Cup and we'll skate it around the ice."

But the fans had scrambled out of their seats and were all over the rink, hugging us and grabbing at our jerseys. We never got to skate that victory lap.

Back in the locker room, we sipped champagne from the Cup as the room filled up with writers and with families. I remember crying, just a little.

When I played for Toronto, I sometimes had a couple of drinks with Dave Keon, who was a heckuva player. In those days we'd always be talking about the Stanley Cup. I remember him telling me that if you win the Cup, you own the city. You know how when you warn a kid not to touch a hot stove, but he doesn't believe it until it happens? Well, that's the way it was for me. We won the Cup, the parade was incredible, and for 37 years Dave was right—people never forgot, and they never stopped wanting to buy us a drink.

You couldn't buy the feeling we had with $100 million.

If you want to succeed in life, you have to have a purpose. How can you dream if you don't have purpose? That's what kept me going all those years. It is like the sun in the universe—it never moves. The planets revolve and are always moving. Goals take you in different directions. I played for Niagara Falls and then for Boston, the Flyers, Toronto, and then the Flyers again. And, except for the time with the Blazers, my goal never changed. It was to win the Stanley Cup.

The celebration was incredible. It felt so powerful, like we could have walked on water.

When you win, it's not just your own city, your state, or the United States of America that notices. It's the whole cockeyed world. You are a member of a championship team.

They awarded me the Conn Smythe Trophy unanimously as the most valuable player of the playoffs. Guidolin said they should have given it to Clarke, and maybe he was right. Clarke himself disagreed. He told people, "The Flyers are a bunch of guys who bust their rears in order to get the most out of their ability. Bernie Parent is no exception, except he has the most ability."

I finished 12–5 for the playoffs, with a 2.02 goals-against average. Boston's big line—Phil Esposito, Ken Hodge, and Wayne Cashman—scored 148 goals during the regular season, but they only got four during the Finals, and maybe that influenced the voting.

One other thing (not that I'm big on statistics): they had 38 power-play chances in the series and only converted three of them.

The winner's share was $19,000 apiece. What meant more to me was what Shero said when it was over. He said, "I've been watching hockey since 1943, and Bernie's the best goalie I've ever seen." He also said, "This is the greatest team I've ever seen. It had the greatest courage and the greatest discipline. Sure, you'd get more on the open market for Bobby Orr than Orest Kindrachuk or Terry Crisp…you'd get more for Phil Esposito than Bill Clement…but it takes 17 men to make a team."

Boston probably had more talent. They should have won in five games. We were a team that had only been in existence for seven years. They were the big, bad Bruins.

I don't know what the odds were, but they should have been 50–1 against us. Nobody gave us a chance. It was like the story of David and Goliath. And now, thousands of years later, the same situation—David won again.

Maybe it was because we were younger and hungrier? Or maybe it was because Fred Shero figured out a way for us to play Bobby Orr. Orr was the catalyst on that team, and it seemed like he was out there 40 minutes a game. Most teams gave him too much respect, and tried to keep the puck away from him.

Freddie told Mark Mulvoy, who covered hockey for *Sports Illustrated*, "We've always made the mistake of treating Orr and Esposito as untouchables. As a result, they've killed us, particularly Orr. The referees think that Orr is

God, too. He's not God. And we've got to stop treating him like God."

When we flew to Boston the first time, somebody on the Delta baggage crew taped a note to Keith Allen's suitcase. It said, "Bobby Orr isn't the Pope. Hit him! Think Stanley Cup." Keith left the note taped to his suitcase the entire series.

Freddie said we were gonna hit Orr every chance we got, every time he touched the puck, to tire him out. I looked around and you could see some guys were skeptical, wondering how that was gonna work. And then somebody said, let's give it a chance. We did, and it worked.

Somebody asked Bobby Clarke what our celebration plans were. Clarke said he didn't know where the party was, but that he would just follow Bernie and walk across the water to Jersey.

We all headed for Rexy's, our favorite hangout, but the fans had the same idea and we couldn't even squeeze into the parking lot. So we headed for Compton's in Haddon Heights, New Jersey, and we partied there.

I got home and somebody had spray-painted my house orange and black, with the message, "Congratulations on winning the Stanley Cup." I had to pay somebody to clean up that mess.

I had a drink, went to bed, and woke up the next morning. Was it all a dream?

I walked out the door, picked the *Philadelphia Inquirer* off the lawn, unfolded it, and there were the headlines: "Miracle Flyers Take the Cup and the City Goes Wild with Joy!"

The greatest moment in my life was when Clarke and I held that Cup. And now, they're going to make that moment live forever. The Spectrum has been demolished. And in its place, they've built an entertainment center built around one of the world's biggest sports bars. Well, they are going to erect a 12-foot-high statue of Clarke and me, carrying the Stanley Cup, right there. I've seen the model for it and it's terrific.

Twelve feet high? That's how high I felt at that moment. And now, it's going to be there forever, just like Freddie Shero said it would be.

"SHERO DOESN'T NEED TO HIT THE FLYERS WITH CHECKS"

Fred Shero was an amazing coach, hiding a vivid imagination behind a bland façade. When it came time to get his players mentally ready for the Stanley Cup Finals, he minimized the money aspect, stressing pride instead. "Win tonight and walk together forever" was his simple but powerful message. (Originally published in the Philadelphia Daily News, *April 10, 1974)*

Fred Shero has the whitest fingernails in the National Hockey League. Which is the kind of thing that happens when you've always got a piece of chalk in your hand. Fred Shero makes Cool Earl, the graffiti wizard, look bashful.

Last night's blackboard message was brief. "A self-motivated team makes commitments," Shero wrote on the Flyers' locker room wall. "Ordinary teams make promises."

This is no ordinary Flyers team Shero coaches. He knows it. They know it. No need to scatter $15,000 on the carpet to remind guys how much money they can make. No need to toss furniture or unplug the soda machine or break down doors.

"The playoffs last so damn long," Shero said after the self-motivated Flyers whipped Atlanta 4–1 last night, "that you can't do something dramatic every day. You've got to win because of ability. Some coaches leave things for a last-ditch stand and try to reach them emotionally. I don't think you reach these guys emotionally as easy as you'd reach high school kids. Besides, if I scattered money on the floor, they might think I'm crazy."

Some of them already have that opinion. Crazy like a fox. Shero keeps his players alert by keeping them guessing, and the blackboard messages are just a little game within a game he plays with them.

"Ahhhh," said team captain Bobby Clarke, "I look at them and laugh. I can't remember any, because there's a new one every day. I wonder where he gets 'em.

"Oh, that one time he wrote, 'An oak tree is just a nut that held its ground,' and Barry Ashbee wrote underneath it, 'If you can walk with your head in the clouds and keep your feet on the ground, you can make a million dollars in the National Basketball Association.'"

No graffiti last night. No impassioned pregame speeches. And no uncharacteristic dramatics from Shero.

"My first year in coaching," he remembers afterward, "was the hardest year of my life. I had the worst team in the organization. I had the dogs.

"Guys told me I only got the job because nobody else would take it. Well, I appealed to them emotionally. I told them, 'We are nothing and we're going to stay nothing until we beat everybody….and then we'll be wanted.'

"Seven of those guys went to the big leagues. Look, we worked twice a day. They wanted to learn. And it was a small town, with nothing else to do. You couldn't get away with that now."

Shero is wise enough not to try anything like that. Besides, this isn't a dog act he's got going now. And he's got some playoff-tested people like Terry Crisp, Bill Flett, and Gary Dornhoefer who don't need cattle prods to get ready.

"I played five years for Scotty Bowman," Crisp said. "He was a psychologist like Freddie. He'd come up with things you never thought of all year long. Like a blackboard talk on every player on the other team.

"He'd put the name on the board. Let's say a guy like Tom Lysiak. And 20 guys would describe his strong points. You'd be surprised, how they'd register. Guys would say he has a tendency to go outside on the deke.

"Well, the game is on, and here he comes. It hits you…. he's gonna go outside…so you make your move. Scotty would psyche you that way, and he wouldn't dwell on their strong points. Nobody's even mentioned the money involved in the playoffs. I'll bet you for that 60 minutes on the ice, nobody even thinks about money. Two

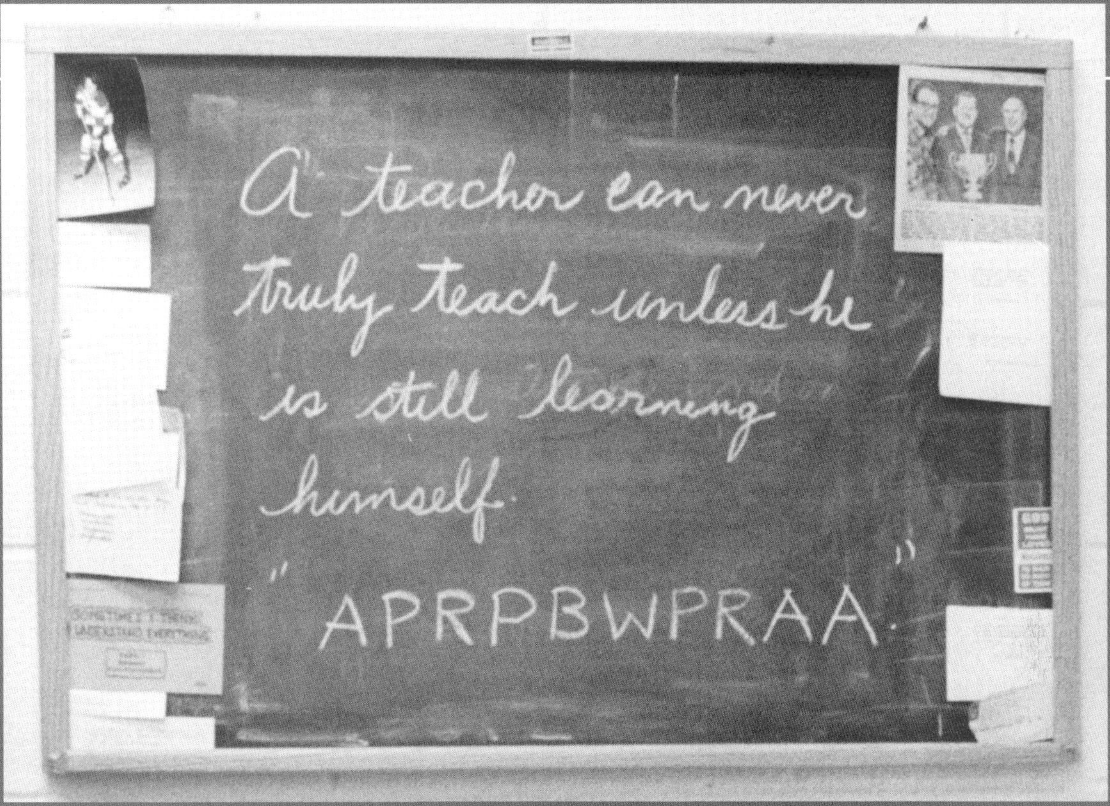

minutes before a game? Maybe. And two minutes after a game? Sure! But not DURING the game."

"I played for Red Kelly in Los Angeles when he scattered the money on the floor," Bill Flett recalled. "He did it two or three times. How guys react depends on how young you are, how old you are, how long you've been around. I don't know if seeing the money helped me…or the team."

"There's something about the playoffs," said Dornhoefer, who played a bristling game and scored the first goal. "I always feel you've got to give everything you've got every time you're on the ice. I owed this one to a kid in Nazareth Hospital, a little boy named Joe, about eight years old. He's not in real good shape, but he's a brave little guy. I talked to him on the phone. I worked hard for him. You forget your own troubles when you talk to a kid like that. He just loves hockey."

So Dornhoefer had his own inspiration last night. And Clarke and Flett and the other guys were skating to championship music they have heard only in dreams.

"Money isn't the thing," Clarke said. "Oh, maybe if you're going for the championship the second or third time, it might enter into it. But for us, winning it, that's the main thing. Freddie never mentioned money and neither did anyone else."

"We had our chalk talk," Shero said, "going over our entire system. Then I spoke for 10 minutes on things other than the system. I talked to them about John Wooden hiding his stars, making Sphinxes out of them.

"I happen to think Wooden is God. But there are some people who say even God makes mistakes some times. Well, I tell my players they've got to meet the public, to take their place in the sun.

"But I tell 'em, don't bask too long in your own sunshine."

Bask too long in your own sunshine and the ice melts. Philosophy, current events, Xs and Os, but not a single dollar sign? "Nah," Shero said. "It would be silly to mention the money. Actually, it's lousy money.

"You've got to appeal to 'em in different ways…prestige and pride. I remind 'em, your record will live forever. The money's not gonna last forever."

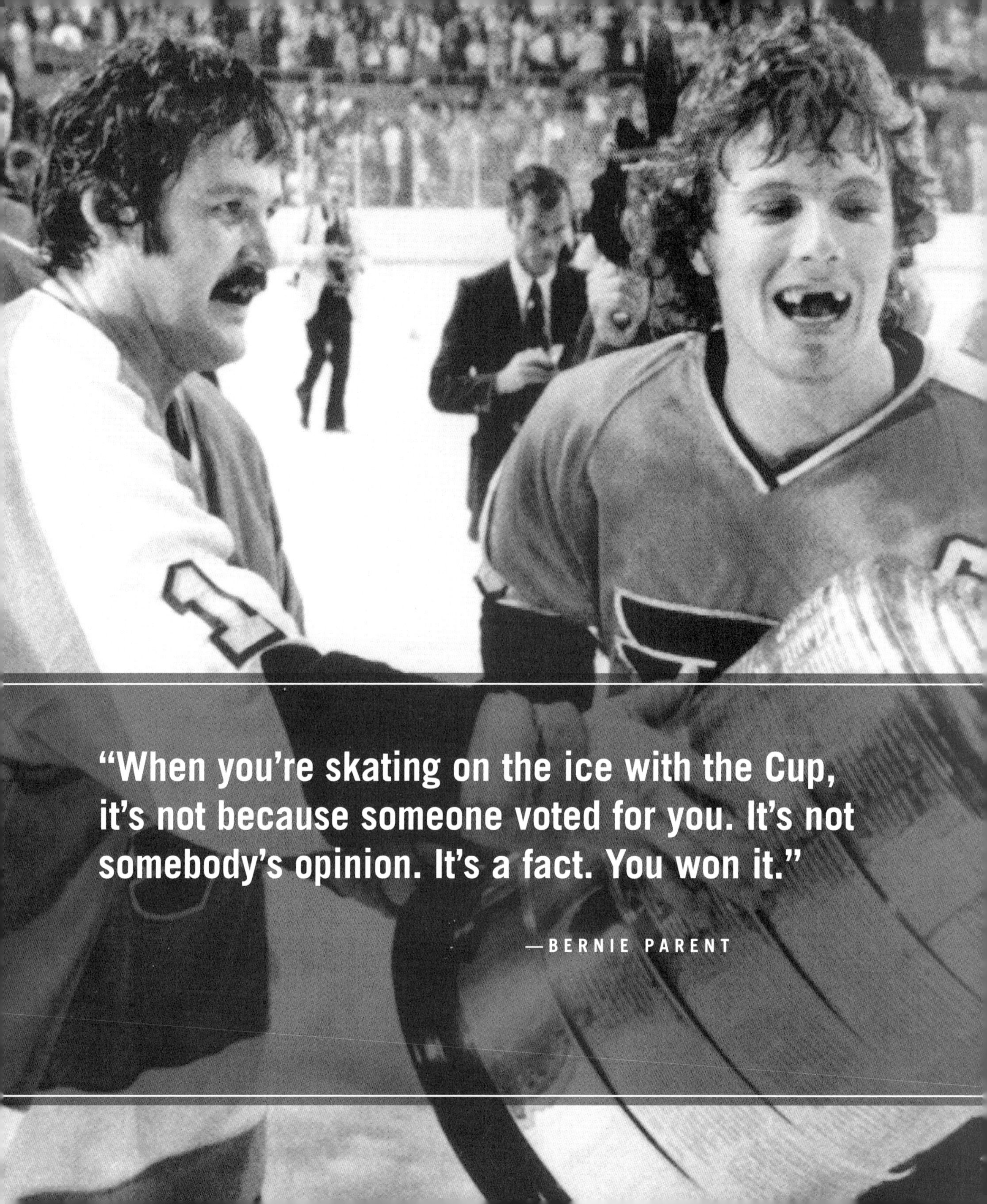

“When you’re skating on the ice with the Cup, it’s not because someone voted for you. It’s not somebody’s opinion. It’s a fact. You won it.”

—BERNIE PARENT

CHAPTER FIVE

DÉJÀ VU ALL OVER AGAIN

Before the next season began, the Flyers gave me and Bobby Clarke lifetime contracts. It was something that made sense to everybody. Mr. Snider, Keith Allen, my agent, and I gathered to listen to the details. We're not talking about millions of dollars, the sort of salaries they make today.

Mr. Snider said it was not a lifetime contract—it was a lifetime *payout*. He said that Bobby and I were the backbone of the team. He wanted stability, and players want security.

He said I already had a good contract, and that was true. He said that I'd already faced as much pressure as anybody, going to the other league and then leaving during the playoffs.

He reminded people that when the Flyers got me back they traded away Doug Favell, who was very popular, and that I got jeered the first time on the ice in that first exhibition game.

And then, opening night, we got the shutout with me in goal, against Favell and Toronto. He said that showed I could handle pressure.

I was 29. My philosophy of life is, you're dead for a long time. Go out, work hard, and then enjoy yourself. You work hard to accomplish things, and once you do that, allow yourself to feel the satisfaction for what you've done.

I felt God had given me talent—it was up to me to use it as best I could. I figured if I got to be 38 or 39 and I was done, I'd be able to look back and say I gave it everything I had. And then, hey, it would be time to relax and enjoy life.

I had to play for six more years. The whole thing was insured by Lloyds of London. There was a salary for as long as I played, and another, lesser salary for the rest of my life. Those first couple of years in Philadelphia we drew about 4,000 or 5,000 fans. By the time we became the Broad Street Bullies, we were filling the place, and 17,007 came out every night.

The lifetime contract allowed the team to spread out the payments over many years, instead of giving me big chunks up front. It made it easier for the team to fill out the roster.

People kept asking me whether having that much financial security would affect my play. It never entered my mind.

When I played, I hated to lose. I loved that the games came quickly enough so that the next night or the night after you could do something about that losing feeling. Being secure didn't mean anything as far as performance went. I had a house in Cherry Hill. I had a summer house in Wildwood. I had a good, 45-foot boat. But there was nothing like winning a hockey game. So the lifetime deal was good for me and for the team, with the money spread out so it would be there down the road.

I didn't care about being the highest-paid goalie in the league. I just wanted to get paid what I thought I was worth. Back in the day they didn't publish salaries, so you never really knew what other guys were making. Today everybody knows what everybody is making. In those days they kept it secret. I think the old days were better. You didn't have all the envy, the jealousy, and the bickering about what somebody else on some other team was making. That shouldn't have any effect on you or the way you played.

It's fun when you win a championship—you own the city, as well as a good part of the world. That feeling carries you through the off-season.

I was anxious to see if we still had that winning feeling when we gathered for training camp. We did.

We wanted to get back there again. We'd reached a peak, and had the chance to slide emotionally, to relax and unwind. Then it was time to go to work to start the climb back to the top again.

We had made some changes. Keith Allen went after Reggie Leach. Leach had played on some bad teams where he didn't have the chance to show his skills. We got him from the California Golden Seals, a team that was being run by the league. Allen offered our first draft choice and minor leaguers Larry Wright and Don McCulloch. Clarence Campbell nixed the deal, saying it was too one-sided. So Allen substituted Al MacAdam for McCulloch, and the deal was done. Allen said Leach had a chance to be a star.

I didn't know much about him until he got here. Could he ever shoot the puck! There are two types of shots: the heavy shot that goes right through you, and the quick shot. Reggie had the quick shot.

He was a good skater, and strong with the puck. A stone-faced Indian. One time for Christmas I gave him a John Wayne movie. He didn't think it was funny. But once he got on a line with Clarke and Bill Barber, he was phenomenal.

On February 24, 1975, *Time* magazine put me on the cover, wearing my mask. The story was headlined "War on Ice" and it stressed the violent aspects of the game.

The first paragraph talked about the goaltender. "He needs the glove of an All-Star shortstop, the agility of a gold-medal gymnast, the reflexes of a champion race car driver, the eye of a .400 hitter, and the mind of a geometrician. Even then he is nothing if he has not conquered fear, for he lives in a vortex of violence in the world's fastest team sport.

"He is the hockey goalie, the masked man, the magnet for action in a war on ice. As in no other sport, the essence of the game is violence—bodies hurtling, players smashing each other…"

Whew. I don't know about having the glove of an All-Star shortstop. Actually, my glove was probably the weakest part of my game. But they got the part right about conquering fear. Confidence was a big part of my game. I always felt prepared.

We won the Patrick Division that year, clinching it with a 4–0 shutout against Minnesota. It was my 12th shutout of the season, the same number as the previous year. The North Stars only got 10 shots, which was some sort of record for us. Clarke had three assists that night, which gave him 101 points for the second year in a row.

The league had changed the playoff system. We had a first-round bye, then had to play Toronto in a best-of-seven series. The first game was crazy. We won it 6–3, but Moose Dupont got tossed for head-butting some guy. Moose was playing with a busted thumb, so I guess he didn't want to punch the guy until he'd knocked his helmet off.

We blanked them in the second game 3–0. That time the Maple Leafs only got off 13 shots, including three in the first period, so you can see what kind of job the defensemen were doing in front of me.

Bob Kelly wound up the star of the game, bouncing off the boards and opposing players, creating chances for Terry Crisp, a typical Hound performance.

We shut them out in the third game 2–0 and someone figured out I hadn't given up a goal in 140 minutes. Toronto hadn't scored an even-strength goal in the series.

We had to go to overtime to complete the sweep, and this time it was Dave Schultz setting up Moose Dupont for the winning goal in the 4–3 clincher. The writers remembered that he'd scored an overtime goal the previous year that clinched the series against Atlanta.

Maybe Freddie Shero remembered too, and that's why he sent Schultz out there early in the overtime. "I thought maybe Schultz could make something happen again," Fred said afterward.

On the flight home, we got to listen to Dave's record for the first time. Yep, somebody had the courage to let Schultz sing on a 45-rpm record. "Penalty Box" on one side and "For You" on the flip side.

What did I think? As a singer, Schultz was a terrific fighter.

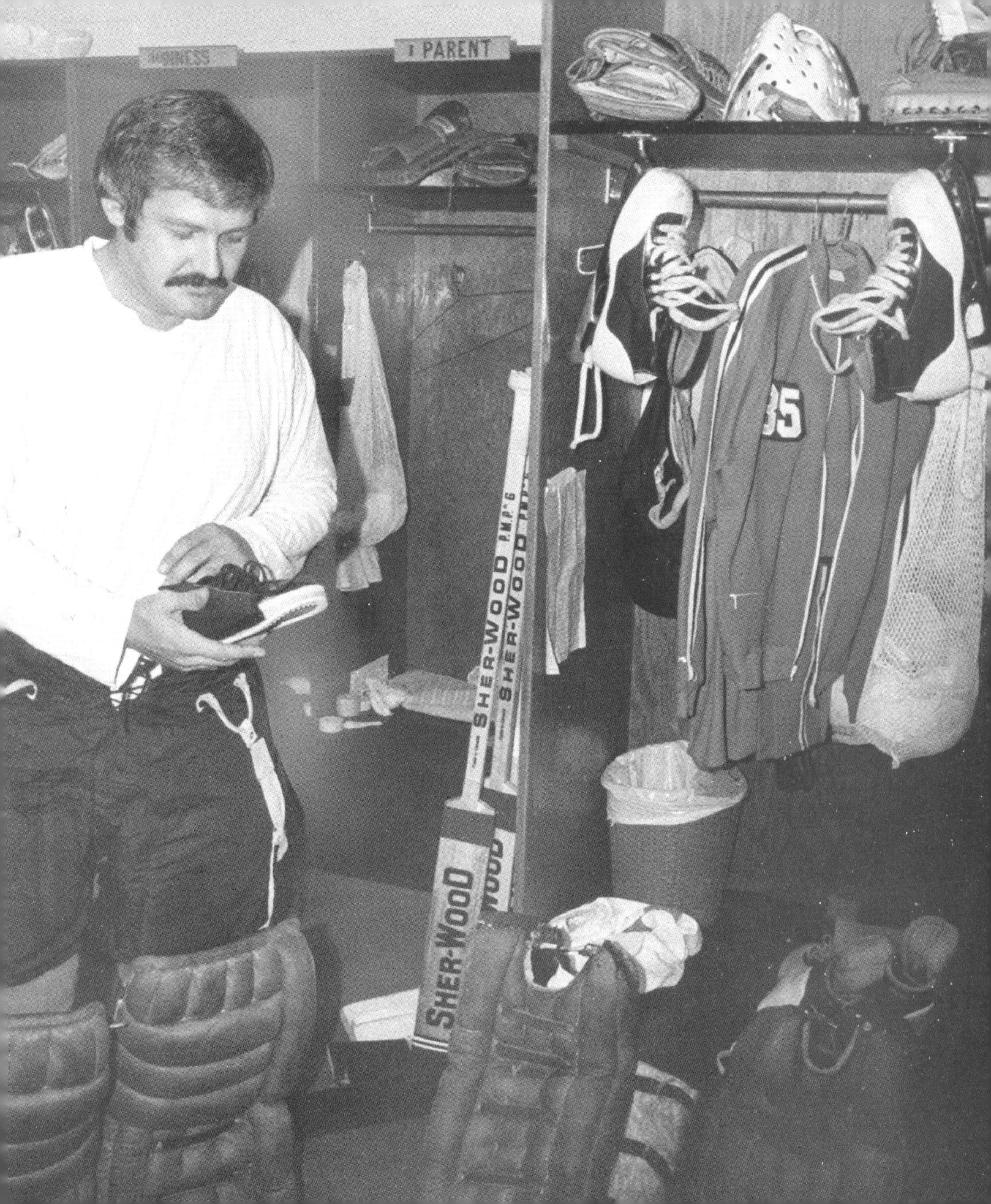
PARENT
SHER-WOOD
SHER-WOOD
SHER-WOOD
35

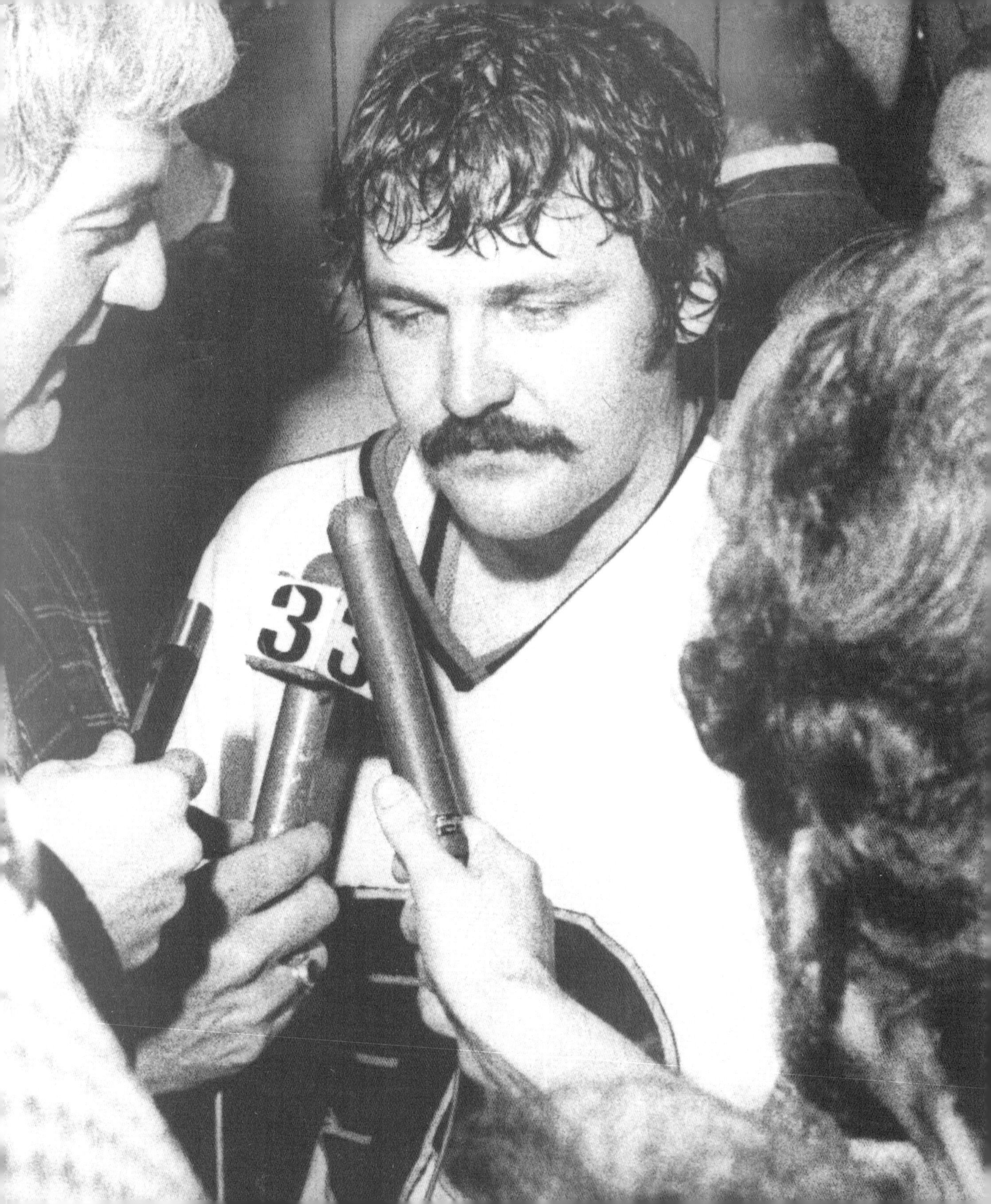
33

We had nine days off before we met the Islanders in the semifinals. I hurt my neck in a Sunday morning practice before the series even started. I wanted to play, so I went out there for the pregame warmup. I really felt terrific warming up. The pinched nerve wasn't bothering me. I was bobbing up and down. I felt ready. That's when Garry Dornhoefer hit me in the knee with a shot.

My stick got caught in my pads, and as I turned, the knee was exposed. So Wayne Stephenson went in and we shut them out 4–0. Wayne hadn't played in 50 days, and had only started 10 games all year. They asked him what ran through his mind when I flopped on the ice after Dorny hit me in the knee.

"Get up, Bernie, get up," he said.

In Game 2, Stephenson was out there again, and this one went to overtime before we won 5–4. We actually blew a 4–1 lead, which is something we hardly ever did.

The game ended in controversy. The Islanders claimed that Bobby Clarke had kicked in the game-winning goal. Bobby admitted that the puck hit his skate and changed direction, but said that he didn't kick it in.

I threw away the crutches before the third game and we went out and beat them 1–0 on Reggie Leach's goal in the first minute of the third period. I only had about three tough saves the whole game.

The Islanders had also fallen behind 3–0 to Pittsburgh in the quarterfinals only to win four straight, just the second time in NHL history a team had done that. Instead of writing on the blackboard, Shero mimeographed a message for every player before Game 4. It said, "No horse ever gets anywhere until it's harnessed; no steam or gas ever drives anything until it's confined; no Niagara ever turns into light and power until it is tunneled." Whew!

The Islanders got off to a 3–0 lead, we rallied to tie it, but then lost in overtime 4–3. We thought we'd won the game on Reggie Leach's shot with one second left. But the officials said the green light that signified the end the game went on before the red light did.

They thumped us the next game 5–1. Bob Nystrom, who was 0-for-44, scored a goal in the third period. Then they evened the series at three games apiece, beating us 2–1 in Game 6. Chico Resch played great for them that

ONLY JESUS SAV

MORE THAN BERNIE

game and stretched our power-play drought to 0-for-19.

If things weren't bad enough, as if we needed another bad omen, Rexy's Bar burned down.

Rexy's was our hangout in Haddonfield, New Jersey, the place we headed after every home game, win or lose. It all started with Clarke becoming good friends with the owner. After a while, they set aside a room, Clarke's room, and that's where we gathered after games.

It became our place to unwind, a place where we could have a few beers. It was a hideout for us. Everybody was sort of required to go there, even if it was for only one drink.

We were family on the ice, and this was part of being family off the ice. Sure, there were other people in the place. Some were of the female persuasion. It was open to the public. People knew we'd be there.

We'd have fun. Back then, nobody talked about finances, about investments. Nobody had that kind of money. What we talked about was winning championships. You don't always get what you want, but you always get what you attract.

When we lost, we talked it over as a team. We talked about how to eliminate mistakes we'd made. When young kids ask me if there's anything I can tell them that might help them, I always tell them to remember the goals they give up. Then recreate that situation in practice, overcome whatever weaknesses you have, and make yourself a better player.

Rexy's was like a clubhouse for us, a place for our group therapy. It was a sawdust-on-the-floor kind of place for the guys.

Nobody could figure out who burned it down. Maybe it was one of the wives. Maybe a couple of wives.

The next day we wore black armbands in Rexy's honor.

The day before Game 7, they gave me a trophy and a check for $10,000 for being named the most efficient goaltender in the league. I wanted them to change the date, but they said it was too late.

They asked Clarke if he thought the ceremony bothered me. He told the writers, "Nah, not Bernie. He was as crazy as ever.

He's going around moaning that gas for the boat is up to 75 cents a gallon. He says he'll take us all out on the boat but we have to buy the gas and bring our own beer. Next thing you know, his wife will be selling sandwiches on the boat."

Freddie was calm, as always. He never changed. He once said he was like a duck—calm on the surface and paddling like crazy underneath. He set the tone.

The night before the game, we stayed at Stouffer's in Valley Forge. Father Casey was there. He told everyone he was not an expansion chaplain, that he'd been with the Blackhawks for 14 years. He said the people in his parish had asked him to pray for us. He said he didn't do that. What he prayed for was that no one wound up in intensive care. He told them that if they wanted to pray for us, that would be okay.

We had a hunch Kate Smith would be there, in person. Someone asked Freddie what that would mean to the Flyers. He said, "If it really means something, I think we should put her on the payroll. I like the song, but it won't put the puck in the net."

Kate sang. And then we put the puck in the net, three times in the first seven minutes. We wound up winning 4–1, with Rick MacLeish getting the hat trick.

The Islanders didn't have a prayer after Kate Smith fired up the crowd and Gary Dornhoefer scored 19 seconds into the game. We swarmed all over them and I only faced 15 shots the whole game.

We celebrated, but just a little—after all, we were in the Finals for the second year in a row.

This time we would be facing Buffalo. The Sabres had been off for a week after they beat Montreal in the semifinals. They hadn't beaten us in 10 straight games, but we knew from the year before that those regular season numbers don't mean anything once the playoffs start. They had a terrific line called the French Connection: Gil Perreault, Rick Martin, and Rene Robert.

I hadn't felt sharp those last three games against the Islanders, and I know I didn't look sharp. So the next couple of days I worked harder. The morning of Game 1, I had a half-hour workout and faced a ton of shots.

We got off to a slow start and it was scoreless after two periods. They put a lot of pressure on us. I think they had five or six power-play chances, maybe even a 5-on-3, for about a minute. But we caught a few breaks and survived.

The only goal they got was on a Rick Martin shot in the third period. I said afterward, "I told the post to take that shot. It wouldn't."

Hey, I made some crazy statements, but I thought of the posts as part of my family. And, from time to time, they helped me out. If you believe in something, sometimes it becomes reality.

The second game was strange. We had a 1–0 lead and then Jerry Korab tied it up early in the third period. They didn't get another shot on the goal after that—a drought of almost 18 minutes. Clarke scored the game-winner on a power-play goal. We had defended the home-ice advantage and took a 2–0 series lead off to Buffalo.

That's when the series got crazy. The third game featured both a bat and fog. Uh huh. A flying rodent whizzed by and I took a swing at it with my stick and missed. Then Jim Lorentz killed it. Guys were shocked when Rick MacLeish picked it up off the ice and took it over to the boards with everybody screaming at him about the danger of rabies.

If that wasn't bad enough, next came the fog. The temperature outside was in the high 70s. In the stands, it must have been 90. On the ice, it felt like 110. And inside my mask, it felt like 130.

Buffalo Auditorium was one of those old buildings that didn't have air conditioning. It was hot outside and hotter inside the building, so fog built up quickly. We had to stop every few minutes as guys skated around the rink with sheets to get rid of the fog. It was tough on the fans and the announcers, but it really wasn't that bad on the ice.

For me, I was completely focused on winning the Stanley Cup. When I got into that frame of mind, it was like I had blinders on. Nothing should bother me, including fog inside the arena. You do what you have to do. The fog

THOSE FIRST COUPLE OF YEARS IN PHILADELPHIA WE DREW ABOUT 4,000 OR 5,000 FANS. BY THE TIME WE BECAME THE BROAD STREET BULLIES, WE WERE FILLING THE PLACE, AND 17,007 CAME OUT EVERY NIGHT.

—BERNIE PARENT

was at both ends of the ice, after all, so the other goalie had to deal with it, too. Years later, people talk about it like it was dark. It wasn't.

From the time you're a young goalie, you're trained to figure out where the puck is going by watching the motion of the stick.

With the fog, I could only see from the waist up, so on long shots, I had no idea where the puck was going.

We wound up playing overtime and lost 5–4 on a shot by Rene Robert. I saw that one. It was the shot before that, from the red line, that I didn't see. Perreault shot the puck into the corner on my left side. He was on his backhand. We'd prepared for this. We knew we had to back-check and pick up the trailers. Perreault came across the red line and shot the puck into the corner. It ricocheted off the back boards to where Robert was standing. He took the shot, hit the corner, and scored.

The way we dealt with the French Connection was another example of Freddie Shero's coaching. Martin and Robert were both great wingers with great shots. They always put themselves in the right position. But Freddie was a master at analyzing the opposition. Perreault would come down the left side and skate across the blue line. He was a left-handed shot, so he'd come into your zone and fire off his backhand. Freddie decided to let him do what he does best: go along the boards, cross the blue line, and try his backhand.

We knew he wasn't going to score that way. If we picked up the trailer, we'd be okay. So our guys let him make his move, he'd wind up in the corner, and we'd pick up the trailer. We used a lot of guys to shadow him and it worked, except for that one time in the fog.

They beat us 4–2 in Game 4 to tie the series at two games apiece. They'd been 1-for-12 on the power play up to that point, but Korab scored on a 50-footer and then Perreault got one, too.

There was confusion about what time the fifth game would start back at the Spectrum, so they went to Marcel Pelletier to make sure. He said, "It all depends on what time the fog lifts."

Once the game started, we jumped to a quick lead and made it stick for a 5–1 victory. Dave Schultz had two goals, which was amazing because he had gone two months without a goal. Freddie was very unhappy with the way we played after we got the big lead, however. When we headed back to Buffalo, we found ourselves in a different hotel, out near Niagara Falls. Freddie didn't like the first place; he said there were too many fans, too much noise, and too many distractions.

Terry Crisp used to say that he'd watch me in warmups to see what I was up to. He said that if I was chattering and moving around a lot, that was a good sign. He saw me tapping my stick against the posts a couple of times before Game 6, chuckling a couple of times, and said that I even threw a couple of pucks to the crowd.

We won that sixth game 2–0 to claim our second Stanley Cup. Bob Kelly scored the first goal on one of his typical pinball, hit-everything-that-moves shifts. Clarke got the assist because he passed him the puck while he pinned King Kong Korab behind the net. Korab was 50 pounds heavier than Clarke and about five inches taller. Bill Clement got the second goal after a terrific pass from Orest Kindrachuk. Orest got him the puck a split second before Korab slammed him into the boards. Kindrachuk told people he watched Clement's goal from the fifth row of seats. (It was the last goal Clement scored for the Flyers because he got traded right after the Finals. The trade had been agreed to—they just hadn't told Clement. He's now a terrific hockey announcer.)

This time we got to skate the Cup around the rink, which is what you dream about as a little kid.

When you're skating on the ice with the Cup, it's not because someone voted for you. It's not somebody's opinion. It's a fact. You won it.

The Buffalo players were kind afterward. Korab told Ray Didinger, "Parent beat us, it's as simple as that. He played unbelievable. The way he was playing we could have stayed out there all night and taken 300 shots and not scored.

We could have shot bullets and he would have stopped them, too.

"What's that they say in Philadelphia? Only the Lord saves more than Bernie Parent? Hah, God should have a season so good."

What my teammates had to say meant more to me. The writers even squeezed a quote out of Freddie. He said, "It was better this year than last. We snuck up on people last season. This year we had no element of surprise."

They gave me the Conn Smythe Trophy for the second year in a row, the first time that had ever happened. The photographers kept pestering me to pose with the Smythe Trophy. I got angry, which is not my style. I told them that if they wanted to take my picture with a trophy, they should take one with me and the bleeping Stanley Cup, which is what the game is all about.

I sipped soda and let the other guys gulp champagne and spray it around. You know what was amazing? Our nickname was the Broad Street Bullies, but if you look at the playoffs, we did not goon it up. During the six games against Buffalo, what were there, two fights? We just played sound, clean hockey. Terry Crisp said it best in *Sports Illustrated*: "When people think of hockey, they think of everything being graceful and flowing. The Flying Frenchmen, the French Connection. Then we came along. They used to call us goons because we weren't very fancy, but now they have no excuses, none, because there was no gooning in these playoffs.

"Put it this way, the point we proved is that a working man's hockey team can win."

It was different this time. The previous year we were in the clouds. The second year,

The parade started at 11:00 AM, and this time they announced the crowd at 2.3 million, which means 300,000 more people turned out than the previous year.

we understood the system better, and we knew exactly what we were doing.

They say it's not the same the second time around. They're wrong. It's twice as good.

The writers kept asking if I was nervous before the game. I told Frank Dolson of the *Inquirer* that I knew some goalies threw up before every game and some end up in a nuthouse. I played each game like Doris Day sings, "Que Sera, Sera." Whatever will be, will be.

It's when a goalie starts letting the game bug him mentally, when he gets uptight, that's when his reflexes go. He starts to hesitate. And that's suicide.

Dolson wrote something next that was weirdly prophetic. He wrote, "Bernie Parent tends goal like an alcoholic taking the cure—one slow step at a time, never looking too far ahead."

One of my fondest memories of that second championship was the plane ride home from Buffalo. It was a charter flight, and they put the Stanley Cup right in the middle of the aisle.

Ordinarily, I'd sit in the back of the plane with the boys and drink a beer. But this time the plane was quiet. Everybody sat there, looking at the Cup. Wow, that was a powerful feeling.

As a team, we realized what we had done and we were grateful. We got to the Philadelphia airport and agreed that Freddie Shero was going to carry the Cup off the plane. He argued, but we insisted. And that's how it arrived in Philadelphia: in the coach's arms.

We hung around the Spectrum until about 4:30 in the morning. The parade started at 11:00 AM, and this time they announced the crowd at 2.3 million, which means 300,000 more people turned out than the previous year. It was better organized, with the players on flatbed trucks.

The parade ended at Kennedy Stadium. When they called on me, my speech was short and sweet. I waved a beer can at the crowd and said, "Well, we did it again, eh? So all I can say is, I'll see you next May 27th."

"PARENT GIVES SHERO KEYS TO SUCCESS"

Bernie Parent was given a car after his dominating performance in the playoffs. He turned around and handed the keys to his coach, Fred Shero. It was a generous gift, impetuous yet heartfelt. (Originally published in the Philadelphia Daily News, *May 23, 1974)*

Sport magazine gave Bernie Parent a brand-new car yesterday and Bernie Parent turned around and gave it to Fred Shero.

"I've always said," Shero told the luncheon audience at the Barclay, "you have to be a little goofy to be a coach… but I think my players are a little crazy too."

Shero is beginning to let his feelings leak out from behind those tinted glasses, from behind that stone mask he usually wears. "The last couple of days," he said earlier, "I've had enough happiness to last me a lifetime.

"The first time I was this happy was when my wife said, 'I do.' The next time was when my players presented me with a plaque. That's the first time that's happened to me in 17 years.

"They told me I was the greatest coach in the world. I made a vow then that I would never leave Philadelphia."

So Shero is here to stay, with time out for a trip to Moscow maybe to learn some new techniques from the Russians, with time out maybe for some correspondence courses in law ("I think that the law, properly exercised, can save the world"), with time out maybe for Yoga or Kung Fu or ballet or hypnotism or whatever Shero thinks will help the Flyers.

He seemed genuinely touched by Parent's gift, but it is harder to read Shero than Sanskrit. "He told me," Parent said afterward, "my wife was gonna kill me. I told him, 'Awww, she's already tried that a couple of times.'

"Actually, I told her what I was gonna do. Freddie deserves it. He's the man who brought us where we are. It is one thing to have a good machine…it's another thing to be able to handle it."

Shero "handled" the Flyers machine. Parent handled the goaltending. And now, for his next act, we are going to find out how Parent handles fame and the overpoweringly sweet smell of success.

"He won't change," said Marcel Pelletier, the glib front office man who was once the best poker-playing goaltender in the league. "Look, he could have made a lot more money someplace else. But he came HERE.

"He could have signed for one year and said, 'Let's wait and see.' But he signed for five years. He wanted to be happy and play on a winning team. You can see the kind of guy he is in practice…the way he works…it shows he enjoys the game.

"Some people said he wouldn't win the big one. So what happens? We win 1–0 in the biggest game of all. All along he showed he can handle pressure. Why?

"He's got the perfect temperament for a goalie. Win, lose, or draw, he's always the same. Goes home, has a couple of beers, kisses his wife goodnight, and goes to sleep. He knows he has it.

"Some guys are saying to themselves, 'Don't put me out there in overtime' or 'Don't let me be on the ice when the winning goal is scored.' They have doubts. Guy like Bernie, they can play every night of the week and sleep good at night."

"He won't change, because he's super," said Parent's agent, Howard Casper. "He's just not a pretentious guy. The only thing that could spoil him is if he got carried away, swept up in all the off-season things.

"Some people are mad at me already. Between Monday and Tuesday he had over 100 requests. The guy needs to rest. He has a family. He has a life, too.

"How can he possibly do everything asked of him? It's not right to ask him to pick and choose. No matter what he does it's wrong if he's got four requests for June 18 and he picks one."

Casper disappeared briefly for one of his hurried, raspy conferences with Parent. He was back with a fresh slant. "Bernie says," he whispered, "that they won the Cup with the support of the people and he'll go wherever he can.

"Bernie won't change as a goalie though, because he's the unnervous sort. The difference is…when Bernie is out on the ice he never takes his eye off the puck. And before a game, he prepares, he reviews the opposition.

"He knows which foot they shoot off. That goal Ron Harris scored on him in New York? He shot it off the wrong foot and Bernie was surprised."

Bernie is so unpretentious he has trouble describing his craft. "You have to have the basic things," he said yesterday. "You hear about a goalie who has a good glove. Well, watch one game. He might face 30 shots. How many does he stop with his glove?

"Maybe 10, right? The rest, he has to use his pads, his feet, his stick, his arms. The basic things you need. Then, when you have a bad goal scored on you, you have to go back and see the mistake you made and correct yourself. Don't ask why. Figure it out and do something about it."

What Parent did this year, besides the best season-long goaltending in the world, besides the incredible acrobatic performances in the playoffs, was stomp the knocks about how he copes with pressure. Next, is the battle against complacency.

Parent was weary, his nerves still knotted from playoff pressure, but he handled the whole afternoon in his casual style.

"We've got a young, strong hockey team," he said at one point. "Young enough and strong enough, so the next 10 years, we should win the Cup four or five times."

It was that kind of day.

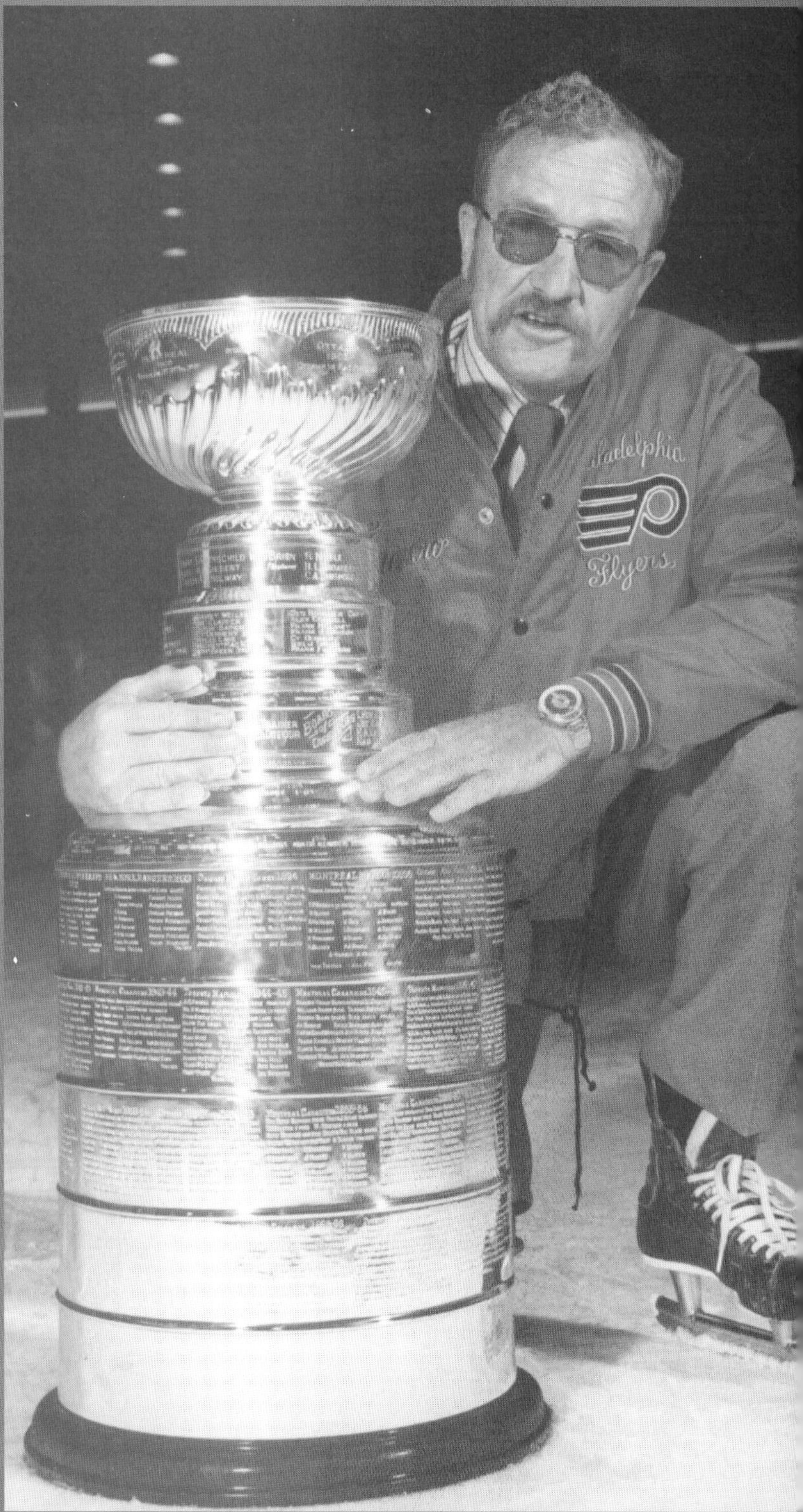

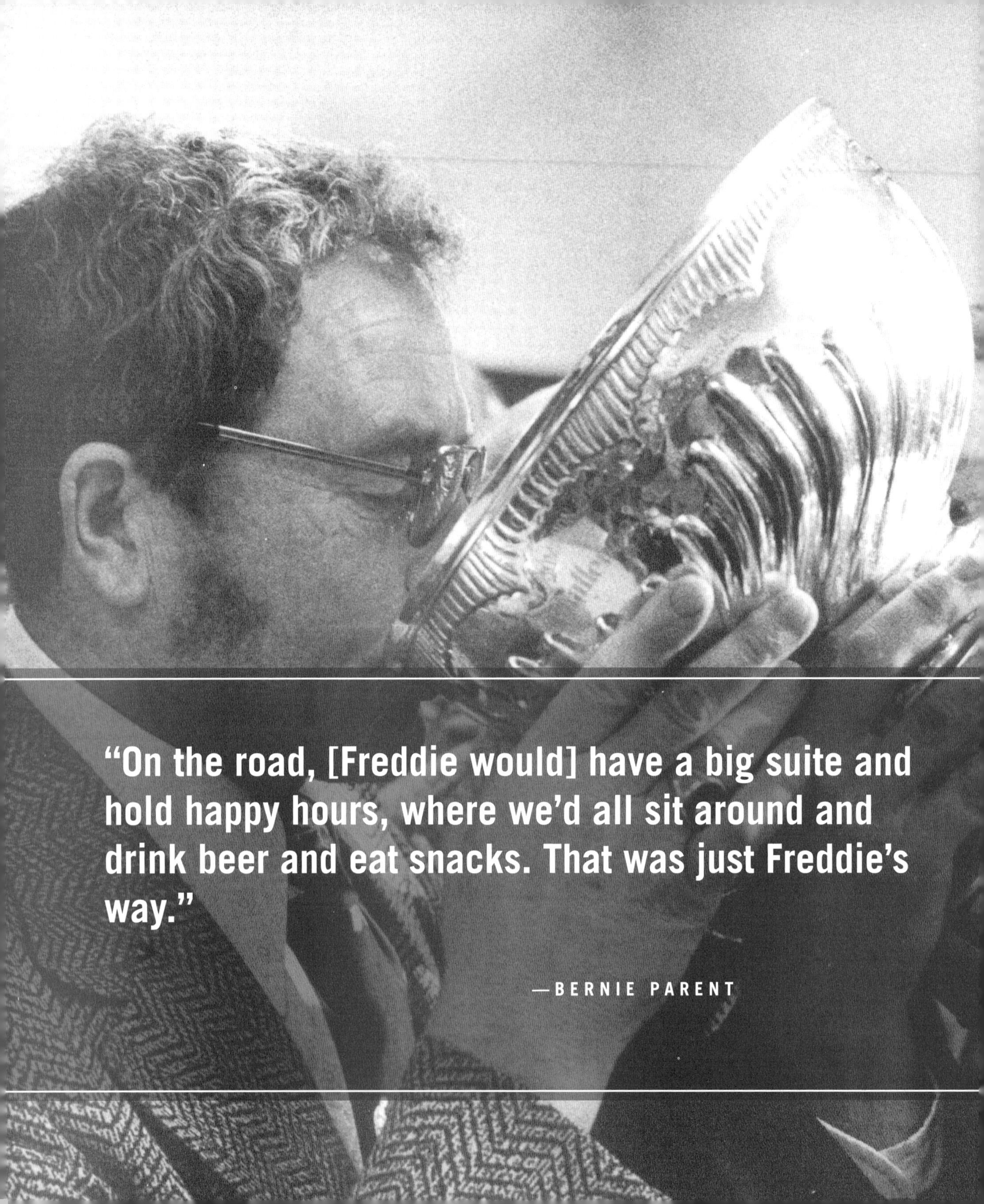

"On the road, [Freddie would] have a big suite and hold happy hours, where we'd all sit around and drink beer and eat snacks. That was just Freddie's way."

—BERNIE PARENT

CHAPTER SIX

FREDDIE THE FOG

We called Freddie Shero "The Fog" because he would vanish and reappear suddenly, seemingly out of nowhere. It wasn't because he seemed confused or dazed, because he had one of the sharpest minds I've ever been around.

When I got back to Philadelphia, he came up to me and said, "I don't know anything about goaltending, so you're on your own."

I loved it.

Freddie was such a big piece of the puzzle. I've always said that you can have a 747, but if you don't have anyone who knows how to fly it, it's not going anywhere. The players were the engine; Freddie was our pilot. We had a heckuva team, but everything had to work together.

What I liked most about Freddie was that he had a system, and it was a system we believed in. We would practice it every single day, which is why we seldom made mistakes inside our blue line. Freddie believed in repetition.

Repetitive practices can get boring and monotonous. Sometimes, we didn't have the enthusiasm he was looking for and didn't accomplish much in practice. So, we'd work on basic stuff and then he'd throw something crazy out there. Sometimes he'd have us work with tennis balls instead of pucks; sometimes he had the guys on defense working without sticks.

He'd have guys sitting in chairs and other guys pushing them up and down the ice. Some of the stuff was really off the wall. It was like he was waiting for someone to question it. And when someone like Bobby Clarke did, Freddie would smile and blow the whistle and that was that.

He was always thinking outside the box. When he got to coach the All-Star team after we won the first Stanley Cup, he talked about adding Dave Schultz and Bob Kelly to the All-Star squad. Lots of people were horrified. Bobby Clarke said that Shero had the right idea. Clarke said that the guys picked for the All-Star Game were always the guys with the most goals. He said that guys like Schultz and Kelly and Jim Roberts in Montreal should be recognized but never were.

I know I personally never liked All-Star Games. They were brutal on goalies. Clarke said guys got to the blue line and knew nobody was going to hit them, so they went harder and really cranked up their shots. At least there's no crowding in front of the net. Stand around and Bobby Orr is liable to break your leg with a shot.

Freddie took some heat by talking about the Russian system so much. He told people he borrowed ideas from the Russians, ignoring the politics involved, the Cold War and all that stuff. To me, it was common sense. If coaches in another country are doing good things, accomplishing good things, why not borrow some ideas? It's not like you're copying everything they did. You're just adding some pieces to your puzzle.

The way I looked at it, we had a combination of North American hockey and Russian hockey, and that made us successful.

Everybody loved Freddie because he allowed you to be an individual and do your own thing. You followed the system, but if you had the opportunity to create, if there was an chance for a 2-on-1, you had the green light to go for it.

It was a great system. Lots of people look back and say we were the most penalized team in hockey the two years we won the Stanley Cup, and ask me how I handled the pressure of us being a man short so often. Well, we had four different ways of getting out of our zone on the penalty kill, and we practiced them all the time.

I probably spent more time around Freddie than anybody else on the team. I had a house in Wildwood, and we had a cottage right alongside it. One summer, Freddie and his wife lived in that cottage, maybe 10 yards from my house.

I had a dock, shaped like a T, that stuck out 30 feet into the water. Freddie, his wife Mariette, and their German shepherd would sit there at the end of the dock, reading books.

He really liked to stay to himself. He wasn't comfortable around people. He would retreat into himself. He wasn't a people pleaser.

Freddie would say he wanted his players to be free spirits off the ice, but he wanted them to think as a team on the ice. He stressed that we really needed each other, five guys, plus the goalie, working and sacrificing together.

On the road, he'd have a big suite and hold happy hours, where we'd all sit around and drink beer and eat snacks. That was just Freddie's way. That way, he knew where we were. As far as curfew went, he believed each player was man enough to go to bed when he should.

That first year back with the Flyers, the race for the Vezina Trophy was neck and neck, me and Tony Esposito of the Blackhawks. It was gonna go down to the last game. Well, I had played something like 44 games in a row, because I loved to play.

I remember when I first came up and Ed Johnston was the goalie in Boston. He told me to never allow another goalie to show what he was capable of because it could come back to bite you in the ass.

I was tired, but we were coming back from the West Coast to play an afternoon game against Boston. It was going to be on national

P.M.P. 5030

TV, and the media was pumping it up and making a very big deal out of it.

So Freddie told them he was gonna play Bobby Taylor in goal. They screamed at him, asking him what the hell he was doing.

Freddie put his finger on the bridge of his nose, pushed his glasses back, and said, "Because it's his turn."

Well, Taylor goes out there and we lose 6–1. I'm sitting there, saying, "Come on, Chief, stop the freaking puck, will ya?" Taylor was my buddy, I loved him. When the game was over, I figured my chance to win the Vezina was too, but I didn't dwell on it.

And then, in the last game of the season, Tony gave up a few goals against Detroit, one in the final seconds, while we beat Minnesota 6–2, so Tony and I wound up tied. We each got a replica of the trophy. The one that stays in the Hall of Fame has both our names on it.

Freddie didn't like that trophy. He figured it changed the way guys played, trying to be too protective of the goalie, playing too conservatively instead of being aggressive.

Freddie had trouble sleeping because he had chronic back pain, which could explain why he was up in the middle of the night the time he got mugged in Atlanta.

To this day, nobody really knows what happened. He was a boxer when he was younger. Maybe he was in some bar and someone recognized him and said something about his team, and a fight started. Maybe he just got mugged walking the streets back to the hotel.

No matter what happened, the fact is he woke up the next morning beat up, so they sent him back to Philly. Mike Nykoluk coached that game and we won it. The Flames went ahead 3–0 before we rallied and tied it up. Schultz scored the winning goal in overtime, which might qualify as the first Miracle on Ice. I know people said Schultz had talent, that he wasn't just a goon. But it was probably his wife who first said that.

Anyway, the next time we practiced, Freddie called us all down to one end of the rink. We figured he was going to tell us what happened, but he didn't. He just said he didn't know if he had been mugged or just walked into a telephone pole. He said that the next time he went out, he would take Schultz with him, the guys laughed, and that was it. We needled him about it the rest of that day, and then it was over.

I remember on one tough trip from Vancouver to Los Angeles, everybody was dead tired. Freddie saw that and told this story about the chicken and the pig.

He said, "You know that ham and eggs you ate for breakfast this morning? Well, the pig made a commitment to that meal, and the chicken made the contribution." Everybody broke up laughing, we forgot about being tired, and we went out and won our next game.

He was a soft-spoken man and a very caring person. That's one of the reasons the players loved him. He had two things going for him: compassion and love.

Many times, he would schedule a meeting with a player and then not show up. The player would start wondering what it was that

Freddie wanted to talk to him about, what he might be doing wrong. Freddie didn't like to be confrontational, so that's how he handled things.

He'd read something in a book and he'd write it down. Then he would put it on the blackboard, or write it on a piece of paper and leave it in your locker. Sometimes guys joked about the messages, but most of the time they accepted them and took the message to heart.

Freddie was very content with just being alive. He was happy to sit and talk with you about things. With him, people always came first. He was the first one to build a nice room for the players' wives to sit in while the players got dressed after a game. He was the first to hold pregame skates. He was the first coach to move his office into the locker room. He was the first to hire an assistant coach.

He figured out how to beat the Russians when nobody else could, and then we went out and did it. They actually skated off the ice, complaining that we were too rough. Mr. Snider went downstairs, talked to an interpreter, and said to tell them they weren't gonna get paid if they didn't get back on the ice. They did.

Freddie made everyone feel at home. Some people have loud charisma; Freddie was quiet, but effective. We didn't always understand him, but we believed in him. *Sport* magazine gave me a car, a Javelin, after we won the first Stanley Cup. At the dinner, I gave the keys to Freddie.

He was stunned, and he said, "I've always said you have to be a little goofy to be a coach. But now I think my players are a little crazy, too."

Funny end to the story. Months later, we were sitting around the house in Wildwood and he said to me, "You owe me some money." I said, "What are you talking about?"

Sport magazine gave me a car, a Javelin, after we won the first Stanley Cup. At the dinner, I gave the keys to Freddie.

And he said, "Well, I had to pay taxes on that car you gave me."

The next year, I was voted the most efficient goalie in the league, whatever that meant. The award came with a $10,000 check. I gave the money to Frank Lewis, our trainer. If you can do something like that to help somebody, to bring some happiness to someone's life, why not do it? I need little for myself to be happy. Sure, I love the good things in life, but having a 40-foot boat instead of an 80-foot boat doesn't make any difference to me.

Frank was an old-school guy. In the off-season he'd go catch rattlesnakes. He'd just grab them and stick them in a burlap sack. He used to make fun of me because I liked to fish. I told him it was a challenge, that it's a big ocean and you still had to go out and find the fish, eh?

He did say some nice things about me. He said I was like a bird dog, that I could sense when there's trouble on the ice, and that I could sense when we were going good.

He put players in different categories. Guys in Group A never complained about injuries or bad equipment. He said Bill Sutherland could have a broken leg and you'd never know about it. Group B was for guys whose complaints depended on whether we won or lost. Group C was for guys who were always grumbling. A guy like Bill Flett—there was always something wrong with him. Frank said some guys were only happy when they had a bandage on their body someplace.

Frank was a special guy. Few people knew that he used to play saxophone in Tommy Dorsey's band. He also played some of the music they used in The Three Stooges films. Think about that—going from playing sax for Tommy Dorsey to becoming the trainer for the Philadelphia Flyers! He used to talk about how the Dorsey band was full of cliques. If he didn't eat pizza, if he went to Horn and Hardart instead of Giuseppe's, he wasn't one of the boys. He said that with the Flyers, there were no cliques. You've got to be compatible to win two Stanley Cups. Harmony has a lot to do with how successful a team can be.

A guy could get laid out, maybe with a concussion, and Frank would slide out there

Frank was a special guy. Few people knew that he used to play saxophone in Tommy Dorsey's band.

and tell the guy, "Come on, don't be a wimp, get up, let's go."

Today, everyone is more aware of concussions and react differently. But Frank was a good guy, and his wife, Helen, was a great lady. We were good friends and he wasn't making a lot of money, so yeah, I gave him the check. I'm still that way today. If I have a surplus of something, I'm going to give it away if another person is in need.

So many times I've helped somebody, and the next day I get called to do an appearance or something for the same amount of money. You think that happens by accident? Of course not. That's just the way the world is.

I remember when they called on Freddie to speak at the end of the parades. One time he told the fans that Philadelphia was a beautiful city, that maybe they didn't realize it but that they would someday. The other time he told his wife, Mariette, that he loved her. Here was a guy who didn't seem to share his feelings easily, and in front of 90,000 strangers he told his wife he loved her. Amazing.

Eventually, things ended badly for Freddie in Philly. He walked away to take over as the coach and general manager of the Rangers. Some people blamed his agent for pushing him into that, but that's not fair. No one put a gun to his head. The decision was Freddie's and he had to live with it.

Maybe that decision has kept him out of the Hall of Fame, or maybe people remember the way the Broad Street Bullies played the game. All I know is that he deserves to be there for the kind of man he was and for all the good ideas he brought to hockey.

"EVEN NOW SHERO CUPS HIS EMOTIONS"

The Flyers won their first Stanley Cup with a belligerent style, but they also had a fiery captain in Bobby Clarke, who played with an intensity that lit up an arena. Clarke played hard, he played hurt, and he gave maximum effort every night. (Originally printed in the Philadelphia Daily News, *May 19, 1974)*

Bobby Clarke's daddy remembered that trip to Winnipeg. Long, scary trip, because the doctors were going to check his son out for diabetes.

"All the way from Flin Flon," Bobby Clarke's daddy said, through the champagne mist in the Flyers' clubhouse. "He'd never seen the bright lights of the big city.

"It was just before Christmas and they had the Christmas lights up downtown. I said we'd take him downtown to see the lights, but he already had his skates on. He was going for a skate on some rink on the outskirts of town. Hockey…it was always hockey."

The Christmas lights shone in Bobby Clarke's eyes last night. He put his arm around his dad's waist and he led him up to the table and he helped them tilt that 35-pound silver trophy and he watched as the champagne cascaded out of the Stanley Cup and ran in sticky rivulets down his dad's chin and onto his gray suit.

The Christmas lights twinkled in Bobby Clarke's eyes, bells jingled in his ears, harps strummed in his chest. A dream fulfilled?

"Nah," said Clarke, "you can't even dream a dream like this."

The Flyers won the Stanley Cup yesterday. Beat Boston 1–0, in a lovely classic of a hockey game…crackling action…frantic patterns forming and shattering…masked gymnasts waiting to smother the puck at either end.

Were Christmas lights glinting in Fred Shero's eyes? All those years in the minors, all those spine-jangling bus trips, and now, hockey's greatest prize, awash with champagne, was in his team's locker room.

Shero stayed in his cramped little office. It was hard to tell what was glinting in his eyes. He wears tinted glasses and he squints hard before he answers tough questions. He toyed with a rubber band and he toyed with a beer and he toyed with the writers. But his voice was bland as tapioca and his face a mask of stone.

Maybe he did shed a tear in the muddle of players after the game ended? Maybe, when he got home, and isolated himself in his den, he took the shackles off his emotions and allowed himself a triumphant shout? Maybe, but probably not.

Shero appears to live in a shadowy neighborhood where someone waits around every corner to rob you of a prize. Don't laugh, don't gloat, don't brag, and no one will steal our joy. It seems like a lonely, friendless place, and that is too bad, because Fred Shero kept this crippled team together and led it up the side of the steepest sort of mountain. At the top, he is entitled to laughter, to tears.

"You're never gonna see Fred show emotions," said assistant coach Mike Nykoluk while family and friends swirled in damp clots in the clubhouse. "He's just not that way.

"Even if, God forbid, Bobby Clarke got hurt and I went into his room to tell him. He'd ask, 'Can he play?' But he wouldn't show emotion or anything. Me, I'm the other way, all emotion."

"He doesn't show emotion," said Don Saleski, who shook off a woeful late-season slump to perform well in the playoffs. "I went in and said, 'Thanks, Freddie.' He shook my hand, said, 'Thanks, Don,' and he smiled.

"For him, that's showing emotion. And I'd rather hear that from him and see his smile than have people jumping up and down, hugging and kissing me."

Fred Shero does not even do that within his own family, jump up and down, hug and kiss. His own son, tormented by his apathy for athletics, rooted for the opposition, until recently.

"I got a letter from a lawyer that pretty much tells the way I am," Shero said, pointing to a letter on his desk.

The letter included the phrase, "I am most happy with my own company" and it quoted from a Janis Ian song about, "Stars, they come and go."

He is a complex, introspective, sensitive man. During the playoffs, he praised New York and he praised Boston. If his team wanted praise they would have to earn it. On the ice.

He would not weave an escape ladder of alibi for them when Barry Ashbee and Gary Dornhoefer got hurt. And he did not encourage them to think they could overcome adversity simply because someone up there likes them.

So much for the "team of destiny" jazz. And so much for Kate Smith. It is fist-swingers, not ballad singers, who win hockey games. And if people are wondering why the championship did not put a smile on Shero's face, he reminded people that he had won championships before.

"In the minors," Shero said, "one year we beat Quebec with only 10 men. I said then, 'This team will live forever.' And at a meeting I mentioned every one of them. And I said, 'We're gonna be the same way.'"

That is hockey they play in St. Paul and Omaha and Shawinigan, the same test of skill and courage. Sure, the skill is greater in the National Hockey League, but courage is not measured by the size of the arena.

And now, having won a championship in every league he had coached in, Shero talked about a series with the Russians, building a new challenge for himself, moments after planting the flag on this mountaintop.

The photographers coaxed him into the clubhouse and posed him behind the Stanley Cup and begged him to smile. "Aw, c'mon, Freddie, smile," they pleaded.

The players smiled their gap-toothed smiles in the background. They knew how much Shero meant to their success. "When he came here," Clarke explained, "he didn't ask Ed Van Impe to carry the puck out of his own end.

"He gave us a system that was good for Van Impe, good for Dave Schultz, good for Bobby Clarke. Everybody could play it. He didn't try to change the players."

"Maybe other teams had more talented athletes," Saleski said, "but we had Freddie's system and we worked, worked, worked. We reflect Freddie's philosophy of life."

The philosophy is laced with hard work. Before the final 20 minutes began, Shero spoke in the tense clubhouse. "Make sure this period will live forever," he said, and they stalked out of the dressing room.

The Flyers played inspired hockey. They respect this complex, sensitive man. The whole town may be baffled by him, but they love him. Aw, c'mon, Freddie, smile. Please.

"There were 17,000 people there, cheering and screaming. And then it occurred to me that nobody was ever going to wear that number again for the Flyers. Wow."

—BERNIE PARENT

CHAPTER SEVEN

LOST, FOUND

After we won the Stanley Cup the first time, I spent four days in Wildwood. They had to have a cop at the door eight hours a day. People just kept coming around, looking for an autograph, looking for souvenirs, or looking to shake my hand.

We went 20 miles off shore, just me and my wife. All of a sudden, along came this big charter boat with maybe 50 people on it. And they're shouting, "We're No. 1! We're No. 1!"

If the back-to-back Stanley Cup years were like a dream, the next season was a nightmare. I played only 11 games and spent the rest of the year rehabbing from surgery.

My problems with my neck didn't come from absorbing one specific hit—they were the result of wear-and-tear, the day-in, day-out twisting and turning that comes with being a goalie in the NHL.

At practice one day, I went from left to right, and I felt this pain. It just happened. It was like somebody stuck a steel bar in my neck. I was helpless.

I went to the hospital where Dr. Simeon examined me and put me through a bunch of tests. They put me in traction to release the pressure on the nerves, starting with a five-pound weight. They kept increasing the weight, until it was up to 45 pounds. Then they decided to operate because I could no longer endure the pain. We knew it was risky; one mistake and I'd be paralyzed from the shoulders down. But it had to be done. The doctors made no promises. Doctors never do.

They did the surgery at Abington Hospital. They found pressure on the sixth nerve on the right side. They removed a small bone spur and a piece of the disc that was pressing on the seventh nerve. Dr. John Wolf said they expected a total recovery.

When it was over, I never worked with any physiotherapists—there were none around. I went to a place in Cherry Hill and tried to rehab on my own. I had no idea what I was doing. Was I pushing too hard? Was I not pushing far enough? If we had the technology we have today, I would have been back sooner. In the end, the operation was a success. It did not affect my playing style, the way I played goal, and I haven't had any problems in that area since.

Those two years we won the Cup, everybody was playing at a high level. It is very difficult to stay at that level.

When I came back, my goals-against average was around 2.35, and the critics started saying that Bernie Parent was going downhill.

As the playoffs approached, there was doubt about who would be in goal. Wayne Stephenson had been playing well for us. Someone told Fred Shero that in the 1964 World Series, St. Louis manager Johnny Keane said he was starting Bob Gibson in the seventh game on short rest because he had a commitment to his heart.

Freddie said you have to do what's right. He said he couldn't have a commitment to me if I couldn't stop a football. And besides, didn't he know that hockey coaches don't have hearts?

Freddie explained that every athlete has to learn to play with pain. With me, he said I wouldn't get over the fear of playing that first game until I actually got out there and played it. He said that once I got over that, the ordeal would be over. If a player goes in without fear, there's something wrong with him.

12

When it was finally time for me to return to the ice, I asked how long it had been since I played. Turns out it was eight months and 21 days. There were 20 games left in the season.

I finally played against Washington, and the game wound up a 5–5 tie. Afterward, I said that at least I knew what I had to work on. The writers asked what that was. I said, "Everything!"

The difference between practice and a game is that in a game, you can't afford mistakes. In practice, if a goal goes in, you can just say, "I'll work on it."

After the game Freddie said that mentally I was ready, but physically I wasn't. He said my reactions weren't there. He also said he had no right to look into the future, that only the devil does that.

The thing is, I felt the same, and I looked the same. My flexibility was still there. I remember a slump, and they brought in Jacques Plante to take a look at me. He watched me for two, maybe three games, and he saw I was sitting back in the goal, not going out to challenge shooters, not cutting down the angles. He talked to me, I knew he was right, and we corrected the problem.

Freddie liked to stay in Valley Forge during the playoffs. We did it again in 1978. We didn't even talk about the next game we had to play. When you're playing a game every two days, it's important to get away from hockey a little bit. So we talked about the Kentucky Derby instead. That was the year Affirmed beat Alydar. I said that if I had a horse like that I'd feed him steak every day. I liked the idea that we got together as a team.

To me, the main thing is to enter a game in the right frame of mind. Do that and you can go out and play your best.

It's something you've got to work at. Maybe you visualize the mountains. The Rockies, something peaceful, something you enjoy in life. Then when you get up the next morning, that feeling of serenity carries over.

I remember Don Saleski used to like to talk about baseball and about the 76ers. If you're at home, any little distraction might take your mind away from the game. In Valley Forge, we were all in the same boat. We felt more at ease when we were around each other.

Moose Dupont had the winner of the Derby in the team pool. Moose said he liked the idea of staying in Valley Forge, talking hockey with his teammates, reminding each other of the right way to do things. Moose was struggling to find the English word for this, so he called it "charistacism." Maybe that's French for "constructive criticism," but then again, I speak French.

The following year, the Flyers hired Plante as the goalie coach and I had a terrific season that quieted the critics. My teammates noticed. Mel Bridgman said that the years the Flyers won the Cup, Bernie was the best goalie in the world. I was hurt during his first training camp. He said that before that, I was kicking out pucks like you couldn't believe. And now that Plante was back, I'd been playing unbelievable. I liked that.

Somebody talked to Jimmy Watson and he praised me, too. He said that when I'm sharp, I'm smart. He told people I played the angles well, and that that came from studying. He said I could see out of the side of my eye. He said I knew where to move, that I seemed to anticipate where the players were going to go, and not just the guy with the puck.

And then it came crashing to a halt one Saturday afternoon against the Rangers. Don Maloney was in front of the net, and the puck was to my left. Then the puck came across in front of me. Maloney was wrestling with Jimmy Watson, who was trying to clear him out of the crease. They lost their balance and Jimmy's stick came up and slashed through my fiberglass mask and hit my eye.

I knew immediately that I had a serious problem. They helped me off the ice and took me to Wills Eye Hospital. I was facing the toughest moment of my life.

For almost two weeks I was blind in both eyes, which was caused by the shock. For 24 hours,

seven days a week, I woke up in darkness and went to bed in darkness. They had to give me strong medicine for the pain.

I asked the doctors to explain what was going on and they said we'd have to wait and see what Mother Nature did. That was not the answer I was hoping for.

They explained that a person has four tendons on each side of his eye that help the eye focus, and that the stick blade had torn three of them on each side. My lens was gone, destroyed.

And then, one morning, I saw a little bit of light. Eventually, the sight in my left eye returned. The writers wanted to know if my career was over. Dr. Ed Viner, who was the team doctor, said that I wanted to be able to play catch with my kids someday. That was a polite way of saying there was no way a goalie could go out there and play with one good eye.

My retina was fine, despite all the bleeding that had taken place. They just didn't have the technology to repair the tendons back then. It was too risky. My depth perception was affected. As Porky Pig used to say in the cartoons, "Th-th-th-that's all folks!" My career was over.

I was not prepared. I looked in the mirror and no longer saw a hockey player, which is all I had ever known. I saw a human being who was depressed.

Of course I was depressed! My mind was going in circles. I didn't have the knowledge I have now as far as asking key questions. That's what the younger guys have to do—ask themselves if they have something they care about, besides the game of hockey, that they would be passionate about doing for the rest of their lives.

It's not a matter of having saved enough money. You could have $100 million in the bank—if you're bored because you're not doing anything productive, you're going to be depressed. Money can buy toys, it can even buy friends, but it cannot buy happiness or peace of mind. My problem was that at no time in my career had I thought about what I would love—what would be my passion—when my hockey career ended.

I never asked myself the question, and so I never thought of an answer. I ignored the possibility because of fear; I was afraid that my lifestyle was going to come to an end one day. It's called denial. Lots of athletes think that way. Today, many players are better prepared for life after sports, but not all.

People had asked me what I was going to do when I was done with hockey, but I never paid attention to those questions. Now, I share my story with the younger generation of players. I tell them not to wait until it's over to start planning. It's a tough challenge, but you have to face reality.

I never wanted to project the image of being too serious during my career. I talked about drinking in a joking manner. I remember when they first came out with light beer. I said, "What is it, 2.88 grams of carbohydrates? I am on a diet that allows 60 grams a day. I guess that means I can drink 20 beers, eh?"

That year I had been drinking too much and partying too hard. Carol was worried. One day I said I had to go to the store and walked out of the house. I didn't come back for three days. I couldn't find my car and had to take a cab to get home. I walked in, went upstairs, and went to bed.

When I awoke, I felt like angels had come down and given me the courage to call a self-help program. That was in 1980, and I've been sober ever since.

I had picked up the phone and asked for help. The program showed me how to live as a human being, not just as a hockey player. I believe that program saved my life.

It's tough to share with people what I went through. For most alcoholics, it's a psychological problem. There's a void in your life and you're filling it with alcohol. When you wake up sober, you feel that void you've got to fill, so you turn to alcohol. It's a cycle that constantly repeats itself. The self-help program teaches you how to fill that void with something else.

There was always a reason to drink—something good happened, something bad happened, it was sunny, it was raining—there was always a reason. Alcoholism is a progressive

THROUGH THE YEARS I LEARNED
TO LIVE ONE DAY AT A TIME, AND
I STILL LIVE MY LIFE THAT WAY TODAY.
IT'S A SIMPLE THING, INVOLVING
PEOPLE, PLACES, AND THINGS.

—BERNIE PARENT

disease. I'd drink to have fun; when I was surrounded by friends, alcohol seemed to always be a part of that. Then you start drinking because you want to forget your emotions, you want to free your mind. That part becomes a problem.

After a bad game during my first year with Boston, I was told to drink a few beers, relax, and everything would be fine. Little did I know it would become something to lean on. Have a bad game? Just drink a few beers and try to forget about it. But that doesn't solve any problems. You wake up the next day and the same problems are still there. I soon found out that you can't escape the memories of a bad game by drinking.

It's just that I hated losing so much. I hated losing with a passion. I loved winning. When we'd win, I'd celebrate with friends. When we lost, I wanted to talk about what we could do to improve the next time, how we could correct the mistakes we'd made. I wasn't drinking to escape.

Through the years I learned to live one day at a time, and I still live my life that way today. It's a simple thing, involving people, places, and things. You have to hang around with the right people, go to the right places, and do the right things.

Today, sitting in a bar is not my lifestyle anymore. Can I hang around friends while they have a couple of drinks? Sure, I can handle that. But now I attract sober people, so that isn't a big problem. If I'm doing public relations and the setting is a bar, I just remind myself to think about what my purpose is. What am I doing there? I get the public relations job done and I get out of there.

It wasn't just the game I missed. You're out there performing in front of big crowds, and then, snap, it's gone. When that day comes, no matter how much money you've made, you're going to miss the excitement.

Money can't buy it. You have to get out on the ice and perform to feel it. You can't replace it. The adjustment can be very, very difficult. I had never faced the reality that that day would come, and I paid a heavy price for that.

The price included a shattered marriage. Playing professional sports involves a lot of traveling, which is something the average individual doesn't have to deal with. It takes a strong mind to be a professional athlete.

There are times you have to put the blinders on. Many times during a season, my family and friends didn't exist to me. You need to be focused to perform at a certain level. And there's a big price you pay for this.

From a wife's standpoint, she has to adapt. It's a good lifestyle. Carol loved going to all of the games. It's an exciting time. Plus, we had summers down the shore with her family, something she had become accustomed to. So, it's a good combination.

When my hockey career was over, I looked at myself in the mirror one day, and I asked a good question. I said, who are you? Wow. The hockey player was gone.

I didn't have an answer. I was 34, 35, and I knew I was no longer a goalie. So I made a decision to take the time and find myself. I moved out of our house and moved onto the boat. And that was the beginning of a heckuva journey.

I was not that lonely. I had so much work to do to resurrect the person I wanted to be. The kids were older by then. Sure, there was some insecurity in their lives because Carol and I had split. But at the same time, they knew I was there for them if they needed me.

I kept in communication with my family—I didn't neglect them and never ignored them.

They were still my first priority. And now, I have an awesome relationship with my kids and with my grandchildren. They will come to the boat sometimes and sleep over. I live on the boat six months out of the year. It's tranquil, it's peaceful. There is something about being on the water that is soothing.

It wasn't always that way. My father-in-law owned a boat for 30 years. Before we got married, I went out there with Carol and her folks. We were two miles off shore and I was sick like a son of a gun. But I've never been sick since.

It was the kids got me started reading self-help books. I learned a lot from them, and that

encouraged me to write my own book about risk and fear.

I realized that there are a lot of people struggling out there. They are lost in the woods, going in circles. It seems to them that there is no way out. I look at my life and think there is something there that could encourage people to find their way out of the woods. I lost sight in my eye, my career was over, and I hit rock bottom. I looked in the mirror, saw a human being, and that was the turning point.

I thought about the difference between the wolf and the dog. I soon realized that the strength of the wolf is the pack. A wolf does not operate alone. The pack is vital.

People have different packs—the people you do business with, the people you socialize with, and so on. If you are smart enough, you get involved with the right packs. You do that, and your chances of success are much stronger. When I was playing, my pack was my teammates, the Flyers. On the ice, they knew they could count on me. That's how we won, with each individual doing his own thing. Off the ice, that's different. Everybody has a different personality.

In the book I encouraged people to take risks. Risks sometimes involve loss. But there are also wins that you'd never experience if you didn't take some risks. I also talked about dealing with fear. Fear is an emotion that helps keep us safe, but it can also be crippling. If you give into it totally, it can keep you from achieving your dreams.

I tried to guide people to find the wolf within them, to push past risk and fear, to not be held captive by fears and anxiety, to become the self-sufficient, satisfied, passionate, and empowered people they were within.

When they took away Muhammad Ali's license to box, he went out and gave lectures. At the heart of one of those lectures was this piece of advice: what you believe, you can achieve.

If you can overcome your fears, you will feel better afterward. When you can conquer fear, you can find your purpose in life.

I will always be indebted to the Flyers organization for the way they reacted when my career ended so suddenly, so sadly. They knew I had no business skills, and they knew I was scared witless about public speaking. They encouraged me to take business courses, and they encouraged me to learn some public speaking skills. I had always been shy. I learned to socialize.

Then they offered me the chance to coach goalies. At first, I was reluctant. Then I agreed to do it. It felt good to work with the guys, encourage them, and make suggestions. I thought I was a good coach, a good teacher, because of what I had learned from Jacques Plante. I tried to put those lessons to work. Was being a goalie coach a passion of mine? I didn't think so. It was something to do, because, frankly, I didn't have anything else to do with my life.

I always tell people they have to find their passion. If one thing is not it, move on and keep searching until you find it.

Working with Flyers goalie Pelle Lindbergh was a beautiful experience. He was from Sweden and he grew up trying to emulate my moves. So when I started working with him, it reminded me of Plante working with me, only now the roles were reversed. I was the mentor, and Pelle was the student.

He was really struggling at one point during his second year with Philadelphia. They sent him to the minors to work things out. I loved that kid and I knew his potential. I told the Flyers I wanted to go with him. So I went to the minors too, rode the buses, and stayed in those small hotels. I did that for three weeks.

The following year, he had a heckuva season. At that time, the Vezina Trophy was not based on statistics alone. They announced the winners in Toronto at a big ceremony. They asked me to announce the winner of the Vezina. There were maybe 1,000 people in the room, the guys all in tuxedoes, and a spotlight on the presenter.

It was a lot like the Academy Awards. You said something about each of the nominees, and then you asked for the envelope. I remember tearing open the envelope, hoping it would be Pelle. I pulled out the card, and yes, it was Pelle. Reading his name out to the crowd was an awesome feeling. There's a photo now at the

0
TIME
0
FLYERS
20:00
ISLANDER'S
BERNIE

Wells Fargo Center of Pelle and me holding the Vezina Trophy. What a wonderful experience that was.

And then it ended so quickly, so tragically. He had this beautiful car, a red Porsche with twin turbos. A fast car, a handsome car. When you're young, you think you have lots of time left in your life, but that is not always the case.

Pelle was out celebrating, got into his car, and crashed it into a wall and was gone. If you'd asked him before he got into that car how much time he thought he had left in life, he would have probably told you 50 years!

And he didn't even have 30 minutes left.

I remember when I was six, and I became aware of what was going on around me. My grandmother was about 60, but I thought of her as an old woman, even then. She would tell me, all the time, I'll be going soon. Well, she lived to be 90, and then one day the angels came and took her. You can't play it safe in life because you don't know how much time you have left. And that's one of the reasons I wrote that book about risk and fear.

It wasn't long after Pelle died in that terrible crash that I walked away from the job of coaching goalies. People thought I was crazy, giving up a chance to stay in the game and to stay with the team. I just felt it was the sort of thing I might do part-time, to help someone who needed help. But it was not the kind of thing I wanted to do every day.

Before the opening game of the 1979–80 season, the year after I retired, the Flyers retired my number at the Spectrum.

It's a long time ago and the details are fuzzy. I seem to remember them putting a red carpet on the ice. They pulled the banner up into the rafters. I still have that banner.

They're retiring my number, No. 1. And I was standing there thinking, *Who am I that they should retire this number?* It's a heckuva question.

There were 17,000 people there, cheering and screaming. And then it occurred to me that nobody was ever going to wear that number again for the Flyers. Wow.

I was standing there, thinking, *Why?* And then, maybe for a moment, I thought, *Why not?*

I think I thanked the fans for their support, and that was about it. Speaking, at that time in my life, was not my strength. If they asked me now, I'd talk for 45 minutes.

In 1984, I became the first Flyer to be inducted into the Hockey Hall of Fame. I remember getting a phone call from someone with the National Hockey League, telling me I had been voted in. You never think about that while you're playing. You want to do well, to play on winning teams, and to win a championship. You don't dare think about the Hall of Fame.

It's been almost 30 years, and how I was chosen to be in the Hall of Fame still baffles me. How did it feel? I felt numb when I heard the news. I called my family in Montreal, my four sisters and two brothers, and told them. I called some friends and shared the news with them.

It's a team sport. Even then, I started thinking about how many players around me had to perform well for me to even be considered for the Hall of Fame. You think maybe they should honor the whole team.

As a kid, you dream of playing in the National Hockey League. And then, you dream about winning the Stanley Cup. But you don't dare dream about individual awards, and certainly not about the Hall of Fame.

My family was there that night after coming in from Montreal. Carol and the kids were there, plus some good friends. Mr. Snider was there, along with Keith Allen and some players. They had a whole table.

Someone from the league spoke first and talked about my career. Then it was my turn to speak. John Brogan, who covered the Flyers for the *Bulletin* when the team started and then went to work for the team in public relations, wrote my speech for me. Back then, I was shy. I wasn't comfortable speaking in front of a crowd. It was a typical speech, thanking the people along the way that helped me.

Somewhere along the way they came up with a list of the 100 greatest players to ever play the game. They tell me I was ranked 63rd on that list, although I have never seen it. You

As a kid, you dream of playing in the National Hockey League. And then, you dream about winning the Stanley Cup. But you don't dare dream about individual awards, and certainly not about the Hall of Fame.

think of all the great players who have played this game over 100 years, to even be on that list is amazing. To be ranked 63rd, that is truly baffling. It really isn't about where you're ranked, of course. It's just nice to be part of a club again.

Sixteen years after that freak accident when the stick slashed into my right eye, Dr. Louis Karp, who was a great individual and a true gift from God, approached me and said a new procedure had been developed to reconstruct my eye. I had gone to him because a cataract was building in my right eye.

He said they could now restructure the tendons and insert an artificial lens. He said he would get the best doctor to do the surgery. I told him *he* was the best doctor in the world and that I wanted him to do it.

The surgery lasted six hours. A couple of days later, he peeled off the bandages and asked me to read an eye chart. My vision was 20/15. Dr. Karp couldn't believe it.

He said I had probably memorized the chart. I told him there was no way I could do that. He said he would try something else. He searched around and came up with a chart that was strictly numbers. Bingo, 20/15 again. He looked at me and he started crying. He said he had just experienced a miracle. Wow.

"SHARP PARENT DULLS BUFFALO'S SABRES"

Fighting is minimized in the playoffs because no team wants to skate a man short against a talented opponent. The Flyers proved against Buffalo that they were more than a mob of hooligans. They had some talented players at both ends of the ice. (Originally published in the Philadelphia Daily News, *May 16, 1975)*

The boxer beat the puncher.

Came off the ropes to do it. Survived a Sunday punch to do it. Sunday punch and Monday punch and Tuesday punch. Spent a lot of time on the ropes early, like Muhammad Ali in Zaire.

Didn't lay a glove on the other guy for two-thirds of the match. Then wham, bam, zam, left the other guy groggy and lumpy, like George Foreman in Zaire.

The Flyers TKO'd Buffalo 4–1 at the Spectrum last night. A ringside poll showed the Sabres winning the first two rounds on everybody's scorecard. Then the roof, which used to blow off, caved in on Buffalo.

Ah, it's probably a lousy analogy, boxer versus puncher. But what's a championship series without an analogy? *Sports Illustrated* would have to fire the guy in charge of thinking up analogies, and there's enough unemployment without that happening.

Anyway, boxer versus puncher is better than turtle versus rabbit or safe versus blowtorch. The Sabres are powerful, two-fisted sluggers. The Flyers are cagey counter-punchers, clutch-and-grabbers. And good defense is supposed to beat good offense every time, on canvas, on hardwood, or on ice.

"Ahhhh, they never used to say that when the Canadiens were winning all the time," Bobby Clarke said after the Flyers had survived in the first game of the championship series.

"I don't think we're that defensive a hockey club. We don't have an Yvan Cournoyer. But we play pretty well in both ends of the rink."

Not last night. Not for two periods anyway. The Flyers played splendid in their end of the rink, which is terrific, because that's where all the action was.

And they kept getting penalized for clutching and grabbing and for hitting below the belt. "We wanted to come out strong," Clarke explained, "but they wouldn't let us. And when they had the two-man edge, that could have been the turning point."

Give Buffalo a two-man edge for 64 seconds…that's like fighting Joe Frazier with one arm tied behind your trunks. That's where Bernie Parent swallowed everything they threw at him, and spit it back out.

Pow, Gil Perreault from the left. Crunch, Jocelyn Guevremont from the right. Wham, Perreault again from the left. Bam, Rene Robert from the middle. Whoosh, Perreault once more, with a haymaker.

Parent turned them all away, catching them on his glove, his chest, his feet, a young Archie Moore. A mongoose against a batch of cobras. When it was over, Parent must have felt he'd passed some kind of turning point.

"Nahhhh," he said, clutching a postgame cigarette. "My best answer to that is that it takes 60 minutes to win a game. You might stop six in a row. But what good is it if they score on the next two? The pressure is always on you."

The Sabres kept the pressure on Parent. He bobbed and ducked and sprawled and scrambled and shoved and only one shot did any damage, a blur of a point-blank punch by Richard Martin. That one landed behind Parent.

"I told the post," Parent said, "'Take that shot,' but he didn't take it. That's what I mean about being careful. You give them a couple of chances and bing, it's in."

There were no more bings. No more bangs, either. The Flyers came storming back. Clarke turned a faceoff into a goal singlehandedly, with the kind of bip-bip-bip moves that Ali would have enjoyed. And then there was an empty-net goal near the end.

Parent stopped 27 shots in the kind of performance that makes computers hum. Like the computer that picked him as the league's outstanding player.

It hummed and thrummed and came up with a 67.2 rating for the goalie. Phil Esposito finished second at 65.7. They gave Parent the trophy and $10,000 last week, the day before that seventh game against the Islanders.

"I kept telling people that I wasn't a leader," Parent said. "We had enough leaders here already. My job in the goal is to stop the puck. That's enough."

Freddie Shero, he never liked individual awards. That's not how he saw the game. He told the writers, "Bernie Parent wouldn't be zilch if we didn't work in front of him. Sure, I think he deserves it. We won in a tough division. We lost a guy like Barry Ashbee.

"Everybody was shooting at us. That made every game tougher."

He was asked if the award was a distraction, if it was enough to make him tense enough to kick the dog. "Nah," Parent said. "Not my dog. If I did, she'd chew my leg off. Kick the wife maybe, but not the dog.

"The thing is, I was so tight. I didn't know whether I was coming or going. I wanted to change the time, but they had set it up far in advance. That night I couldn't sleep. Up at 5:00 in the morning, thinking."

The Flyers won that one, ending a three-game skid. And last night, Parent looked like one of those Friday night fight commercials, "To look sharp, to be sharp, da-da-dum-da-dum…"

"The difference," he explained, "is that I found out I need more work. I didn't get much work before the Islanders series. You lose your timing. The last couple of days I've been working harder. And this morning, I took a half-hour workout. Broke a sweat. Felt good."

Last night felt good too, when it was over. Parent is not anxious to play target again for Buffalo gunners. "Ahhhh," he promised, "we were a little tired tonight. Sunday, we go back to forechecking and hitting. Be a different game."

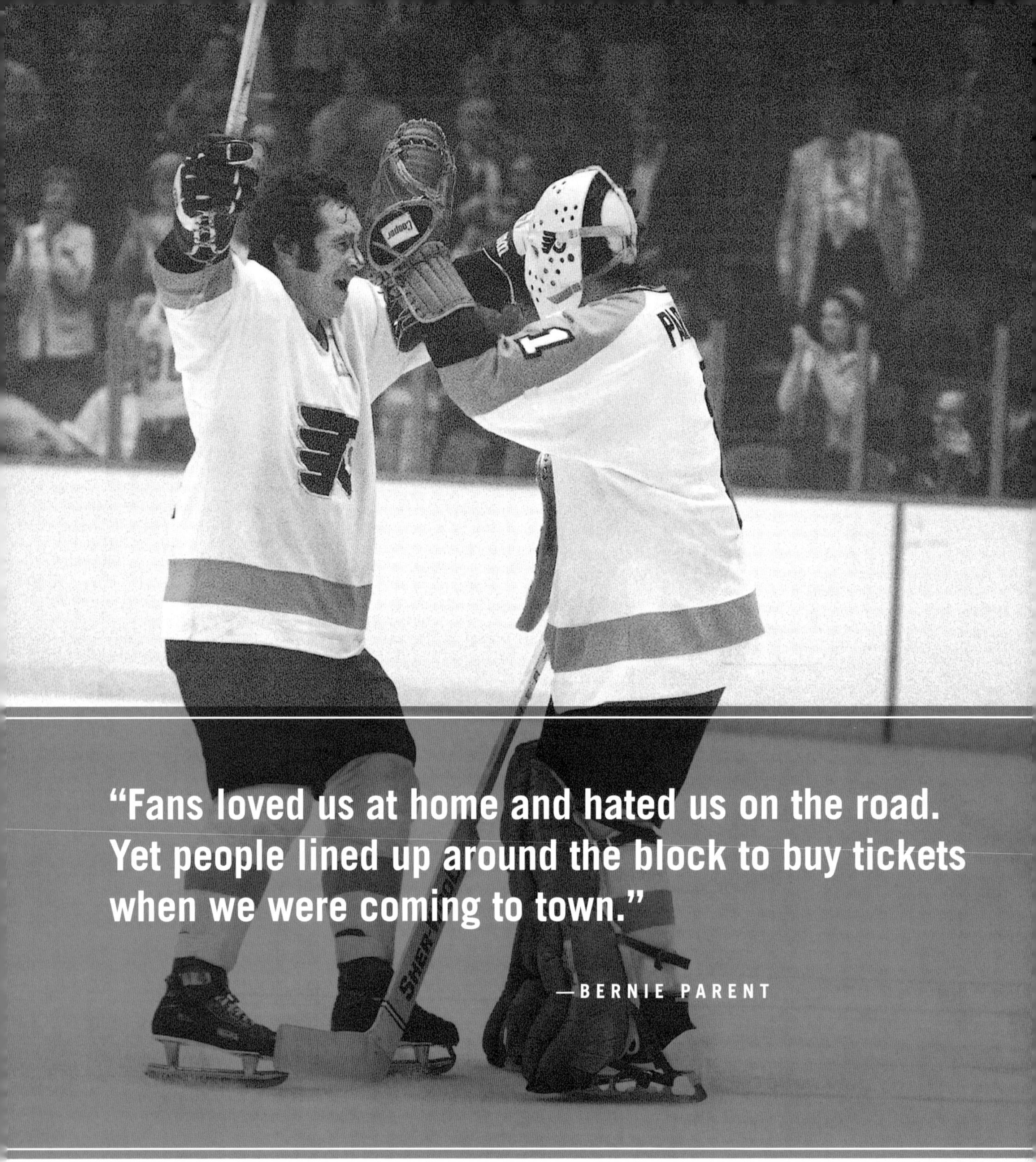

"Fans loved us at home and hated us on the road. Yet people lined up around the block to buy tickets when we were coming to town."

—BERNIE PARENT

THE CROWDED CREASE

It used to be that the crease was the crease. The part of the ice in front of the net—the part that's painted blue—belonged to the goalie. If an opponent put the tiniest part of his skate blade inside the crease when a shot was taken, the whistle blew, and the goal didn't count.

Now, somebody takes a shot, the rebound is out there, and you've got four, maybe five guys in the crease poking at the puck, shoving the goalie, and the referees allow it. Plus, now, defensemen are not allowed to cross-check and clear a guy out in front of their goalie. Someone jams the puck in, and the players whoop and celebrate. What are they celebrating?

I understand the NHL changed some rules to make it easier to score goals because the league thinks people want to see more goals and it wants to make the game more popular.

But at a certain point it just gets ridiculous. Who wants to see a goal that's scored by four guys pushing the goalie, poking at him, jabbing at the puck, trying to shove it past him? How exciting is that?

People ask me all the time what became of the beautiful goals guys like Bill Barber or Rick MacLeish used to score. Goals from angles, goals from the faceoff dots? You don't see them for a couple of reasons. Mainly, goalies have gotten bigger. Add to that the equipment they're wearing and you've greatly cut down the chances for a goal.

If I'm going to criticize the league, I have to praise it when it does something that helps the game. They stopped all that hooking which used to slow the game down and made it boring. They eliminated most of that, and it has made a big difference. Plus, players don't freeze the puck against the boards now, and that helps.

I see some teams today play a trap on defense. That slows the game down. One game, the Flyers just passed the puck back and forth in their own zone. Well, it's up to them to figure out a way to beat that defense. The league can't get involved. It becomes a dictatorship if the league has to settle everything. If they really want to stop it, have the referees call a delay of game penalty if a team won't come out of their zone.

It would make more sense then the delay of game penalty that comes when a team is shorthanded and someone fires the puck down the ice and it somehow clears the glass and goes out of the rink. Rules are rules, I understand that. But you have to apply some common sense.

I'm not happy with shootouts deciding games, but you probably would have guessed that, coming from an old goalie.

To me, it's a lot like football: guys sweat and bleed and struggle for 59 minutes, and here comes a 160-pound kicker out there with 10 seconds left and he boots a 60-yard field goal to win the game.

How fair is that? I'd like to see them have a rule that in the final two minutes a team has to get to the 30-yard line before they can try a field goal. I seem to remember a guy kicking a 62-yarder against the Eagles to beat them.

In hockey, you play for 60 minutes plus overtime, and then one lucky bounce can win the game. That doesn't make sense. You win as a team, you should lose as a team. The shootout makes it an individual thing. It really goes against everything I felt about my job. Somewhere along the way, I came to believe that when preparation meets opportunity, you've got a good chance of doing well. I was determined to be prepared every time I went out there.

My style was simple: I was an angle goalie. That meant I had to know where I was at all times. My system depended on having terrific defensemen in front of me, guys who were smart and tough. I had to know what they were going to do in certain situations. That way I could react and get to the right place at the right time.

Preparation plus anticipation were the keys to my game. When the Flyers first came to Philadelphia, a columnist described the game of hockey as one long broken play. He wouldn't dare do that now. Coaches study so much video and break it all down. You get to know what the other team likes to do once they're inside your blue line. Patterns, trends, call it whatever you want, but you have to analyze what the other team does and prepare to defend against it.

Freddie Shero emphasized playing as a team. You had to trust in the other guys out there. For me, I could concentrate on the guy with the puck, knowing that my back-checker would pick up the guy in the slot. That way, there would be no hesitation, no moment of doubt. I could devote all my attention to the guy with the puck, knowing the front would be taken care of by one of my teammates doing his job.

My philosophy was always to try and make the saves look easy. The best way to do that was to be in the right position. Let the people think that all I did was make the easy save. That's okay. If I'm in the right place at the right time, the save is going to look easy. If I'm not in position and I have to dive to make a spectacular save, the fans might love it but I wouldn't be proud of it.

I was more interested in results, as opposed to style. It kept coming up when Doug Favell and I played for the same team. People loved him in Philadelphia, and I understood why. Favell's style entertained them. When you step

In hockey, you play for 60 minutes plus overtime, and then one lucky bounce can win the game. That doesn't make sense. You win as a team, you should lose as a team.

on the ice, you're playing hockey, but you're also entertaining people. Favell dropped to his knees and kicked at the puck. He was a heckuva athlete and a lacrosse player. He'd make some spectacular saves.

You have to remember, when I came back to the Flyers the second time, they traded the very popular Favell to Toronto. So I had a lot to prove, and that was the first motivation. Then, I looked around and saw we had a chance to win the Stanley Cup, and that became my main motivation.

Let's face it, I had a boring style. If I put myself in the right position to get hit by the shot, so be it.

My biggest weakness was my glove hand. That was definitely not my strong point. That forced me to concentrate on cutting down the angles even more. In my mind, I was concentrating on compensating for that weakness, bending my elbow at a certain angle.

There was a game where I got beat twice high to the glove side. The next day in practice I told the guys I wanted them to shoot high to the glove side. I had them shoot 50 pucks at me that way to get my rhythm back. It worked.

My strength was in my balance, the way I distributed my weight. Toward the end of my career, I finally realized that everything was done from the knees. I could flex my knees whichever way the play was going without committing the rest of my body. The play would change direction, as it often does, and all I had to do was adjust my knees and move my body in that new direction.

As far as stickhandling skill, I learned so much from Plante. He taught me how to come out from in front of the net. There are all sorts of ways to pursue the puck behind the net. If you only used your stick, coming from one direction, the puck could bounce over your stick and you'd lose it. From the other side, you could press against the boards with your pads, cutting down the chances of the puck bouncing past you.

Timing was essential. Your defenseman was coming back at 15 miles an hour, so you wanted to leave the puck five or six inches from the boards. That made it easier for him to pick up the puck. You wanted to try to leave your net from the opposite side from where the defenseman was coming. You'd practice that kind of thing every day.

And in the end, communication is vital. Sure, my teammates and I had an understanding because we'd practiced together, but in the heat of the game, we still had to talk to each other, say out loud what we were going to do, even if it got drowned out sometimes by the noise of the crowd.

I learned as a kid that you had to have a system, and you couldn't let up on the system, even for an instant. You do that, bad things will happen.

I seldom lifted the mask during a game. That was intentional. When an opponent scores a goal against you, you're standing in the crease, and you want to hide behind the mask. There's nothing you can do about it. The red light went on, the scoreboard changed. But you need the discipline and a strong mind to stick with your system, to maintain a positive attitude.

That doesn't happen automatically. You need to be prepared. Short term, before they drop the puck to resume play, you review in your mind how the goal was scored. You think about what you should have done in that situation. Get it done in 10 seconds, shut it off, and go back to your system.

Between periods is when a goalie has more time to analyze what happened, to replay in his mind how a goal was scored. And then you refocus on how you will handle the same situation the next time it comes up, because it will come up again.

People talk about the Broad Street Bullies and the success we had, winning back-to-back Stanley Cups. They say that we could afford to play our aggressive, intimidating style, even if it meant taking a penalty, because I was back there in goal and could deal with us being a man short.

That's giving me too much credit. Take someone like Ken Dryden, who was 6'4" and had a different style. You put Dryden on a lousy team and you don't win a Stanley Cup. He had a great team around him in Montreal. Same with me. You put me on a lousy team, we don't win the Stanley Cup. I do think that in each playoff series, the goalie can steal one game for you. They call it standing on your head. I was never comfortable with that description. I just think the goalie can make all the routine saves, plus a handful of tough saves, and make the difference in that game.

You can't single out one player when you win a championship. It works both ways. My teammates knew they could depend on me, and I knew I could depend on them. That combination made us a powerful team.

There is magic involved. We beat Boston in six games. They should have beaten us in four straight, based strictly on the talent. We had no right to win the Cup that year. They had Bobby Orr, Phil Esposito, Wayne Cashman, and Ken Hodge. It was David against Goliath, yet we won.

That series reminds me of the magic of Christmas. It was like an incredible gift.

Some of the old-timers talked about that during the Winter Carnival, when we gathered to play on a Flyers alumni team against a Rangers alumni team.

We had 13 players and a coach on hand, playing or acting as off-ice ambassadors. We

NHL

VICTORIA

had Bill Barber, Bobby Clarke, Terry Crisp, Gary Dornhoefer, Larry Goodenough, Bob Kelly, Orest Kindrachuk, Reggie Leach, me, Joe and Jimmy Watson, Dave Schultz, Don Saleski, and the former assistant coach, Mike Nykoluk.

Some of the guys were asked how we managed to beat the heavily favored Bruins that year. Joe Watson, the oldest guy to play in the alumni game at 68, said, "First game, we lost 3–2, but after that we knew we were gonna beat 'em. We were playing good defense and that was the key. We were in better shape. And I don't think they took us seriously. They were holding optional practices and Bobby Orr would show up and maybe six or seven other guys. The rest of the team was at Garden State Racetrack in Cherry Hill."

Bob Kelly said, "We had never won up there, so of course we were underdogs. I got knocked out in the Rangers series, so I wasn't a part of it. But Clarke did what he did and Bernie stood tall.

"Fighting wasn't that big a factor. In a way, the Bullies thing overshadowed the talent we had on the team, guys like Clarke, Dorny, Barber. Plus, we had Barry Ashbee back there until he got hit in the eye with the puck. We had Steady Eddie Van Impe. We had the Watson brothers."

"They had the bigger names," Bill Barber said, "but maybe our youth paid off. Freddie used our bench; that's the way he coached. 'Use it or lose it,' he used to say."

We had a great team those two incredible years, but you still had to perform as an individual. How did I get there? I believe in the power of the universe. Everything that happened in my life took me one step at a time to that point. Were they all good steps? No, I got my ass kicked many times. I got traded from the Flyers to Toronto and I cried like a baby. But if I hadn't gone to Toronto and had not had the chance to work with Jacques Plante for those two years, the rest would not have happened.

Plante gave me an understanding of the game. I wish I could have learned those lessons earlier in my career, but I didn't. Plante taught me how important practice could be. I would work on one thing until I felt I had it down pat. It might take months, sometimes even a whole season. Work on something, perfect it, and then move on to something else. My brother, a psychologist, once suggested that I should leave any troubles at the rink. I don't believe that.

I took any troubles I was having in games home with me. I worked on them when I got home. But I never kicked the dog—if I had, she'd have bitten my leg off!

A lot of times, I took my thoughts into the woods with me. I loved the outdoors and still do. After practice I might go hunting—in season, of course. It wasn't just the killing that drew me there; it was the natural feeling I had when in the woods.

If you have happy thoughts, good ideas followed. I'd sit there, waiting for a deer to come into view, and I'd review all the plays of the previous game. Not the saves I made, but the goals I'd allowed. I'd visualize how I would position myself in a different way the next time.

You didn't hear that much about concussions back in the 1970s. If a guy had his bell rung, he sat out a few days and then came back. The thinking was that if you don't want to get hurt, don't play the game. Hockey was a man's game. It was for men, not wimps. And the Broad Street Bullies represented the idea that you backed down from nobody, that you would pound people until they gave up the puck a little earlier, until they applied the brakes a little sooner.

People still remember Dave Schultz, the Hammer, for his fighting. If someone delivered a cheap shot to one of our skill guys, someone responded, and 99 percent of the time it was Dave Schultz.

How do I think he felt about his role on the team? I answer with one word—passion.

Schultz loved it. It was his passion. I look back at the fighters I remember in the National Hockey League, and nobody showed the passion that Dave did. He loved the attention and thrived on it. He had charisma. He wasn't just a fighter. He'd skate out onto the ice with his long, curly hair and that full mustache. He would stare back at the opposing fans, and they could feel his anger through the glass.

SHER-WOOD

We got criticized for our style of play throughout the league. We were the most penalized team in the league the two years we won the Cup. Schultz piled up the penalty minutes. But it wasn't like the Flyers brought some boxer in to teach the players how to throw a punch. They did bring in a martial arts guy and he taught things about balance, about grabbing the other guy's shirt in a way to throw him off-balance, that kind of thing.

Fans loved us at home and hated us on the road. Yet people lined up around the block to buy tickets when we were coming to town.

They were hoping to see their team kick our asses. And when they didn't, they hissed. We led the league in road attendance. You can look it up. Look at it that way and we were good for the league, not bad for the league.

As the goalie, I seldom fought. But I was part of the team and understood our image. I got involved a few times. You skate down to the other end, grab the other goalie by the shirt, and hold on tight. Let's face it, I fought one time. I traded punches with a guy while I was with Niagara Falls, and he knocked me out. I decided I never wanted to do that again.

Sure, I finished the game. I'm no quitter.

I've always felt that the ice surface and the dimensions of the rink are the same, home and away. The only thing that changes on the road is the crowd. At home we had passionate support night after night, and I think it made the difference in winning the Stanley Cup.

On the road, we faced hostility, but the negative reaction made us play well. Me, I loved it. It got me pumped up. Fans hated us in other cities, but they showed up.

I kid Dave Schultz a lot, but he did have some skills. One year he scored 21 or 22 goals, and that's a lot of goals. But he knew what his role was on our team.

Fred Shero never sent him out there with orders to start a fight. Schultz was smart enough to know the situation. There was a purpose behind most of the fights he got involved in. Most of the time it was to get even for a cheap shot. Some of the time, especially early in a game, it was payback for something that had happened the last time the two teams met. And sometimes, right at the start of a game, it was just to get things going, to set the tone. He was smart that way. A lot depended on who was willing to challenge him.

The only time Schultz really got angry was when some writer compared him to an animal. Larry Merchant did that in a column he wrote for the *New York Post*, comparing Schultz to a vicious Doberman. The next day at practice, Stan Hochman was standing in the penalty box, watching the workout. Schultz skated up to him and waved his stick in front of Stan's face, maybe inches from his nose, carving a figure 8 in the air. I guess all sportswriters looked alike to Schultz.

Fighting has always been a part of hockey. Somebody wrote a story for *The New York Times* that traced fighting back to Montreal, where they had club teams based on ethnic groups: the French, the Irish, the British. They suggested that the players didn't just want to win on the scoreboard—they wanted to punch the other guys' lights out to establish superiority of one group over another. I wouldn't know about that. I wasn't around back then.

You have an ice surface that's 85' x 200' with 10 players plus the goalies out there. They're skating back and forth at 25 miles an hour. Collisions are unavoidable.

It's a fast-paced game, a hitting game, and guys will get frustrated at times. That's when fights start.

When someone knocks you down, grabs your stick, and puts an elbow in your face, you want to stand up for yourself.

In baseball you seldom see guys banging into each other. Sure, there are the occasional bench-clearing brawls, but they usually start when a pitcher throws at a hitter because the hitter showed him up the previous at-bat. In football, it's usually something that happens after the whistle, guys doing nasty things that the other guy doesn't anticipate because the play is over. But football players wear so much equipment that you don't see much damage from a fight.

You seldom see a bench-clearing fight in hockey anymore. They now penalize the third man in, the guy who gets involved after two guys square off. But I'm not sure there are any statistics that prove fighting is going away anytime soon. It seems like each team has one guy on the roster who has gained respect for his fighting skills, but also has the talent to do other things.

I'm aware that recent stories have linked guys who were designated enforcers with brain damage, or that later in life they may become addicted to drugs or alcohol. But I'm not convinced that the two things are tied together. I think the league is going after this the wrong way. When players stop playing hockey, the league should have a system in place that helps them deal with the rest of their lives. I think not having a support system in place creates more damage than a punch to the head. And that goes for all sports, not just hockey.

Some people point out that there is very little fighting in the Olympics and say that people would rather see that style of hockey. Hey, the Olympics last two weeks, and then they're over. I can watch an NHL game for one period, sit there for 20 minutes, and all I see is guys skating back and forth. The building is so quiet you could hear a whisper. And then, boom! Somebody throws a good check, knocks a guy into the boards, and the building comes to life again. It creates excitement, and people love it.

Why would they want to take fighting out of the game? Go to downtown Philadelphia, or any big city with pro hockey, and ask 100 people what they think of fighting. A large percentage will say that it is part of the game.

Maybe this would be a good time to remind people that when we beat Buffalo in the finals to win the Stanley Cup, there were only two fights in six games. Two!

During the playoffs, you get low-scoring, tight-checking games. Nobody wants to hand the other team a power-play advantage by taking a dumb penalty or instigating a fight. The year before, against Boston, it might have been a little different. The Bruins were a tough, physical team. Buffalo was more of a skill team, a skating team, that featured the French Connection line.

I praise the NHL when I think it deserves praise, and I criticize the league when I think it deserves criticism. I think they need to take a good, hard look at returning the red line to the game. Players today are bigger, stronger, and faster than they were back in my day, but the rink has stayed the same size. After they eliminated the red line, players could get up a full head of steam and are now skating faster than ever. The game is too fast.

Somebody once explained to me that you can figure out the force of a collision by multiplying mass (the guy's weight) and speed (how fast is he skating). It sounds complicated, but it's just common sense. If you're driving a Volkswagen at 25 miles an hour and you hit somebody else's car broadside, you are not going to do as much damage as you would if you were driving an Escalade at 50 miles an hour.

The 2011–12 Flyers team had speed like they have never had before. But at one point in December, they had four guys—Chris Pronger, Claude Giroux, Brandon Schenn, and Sean Couturier—out with concussions, Pronger for the season, Couturier after being hit by a puck in the back of his helmet.

It seemed as though Giroux, who is a terrific player, was injured by his own teammate, Wayne Simmonds. Giroux was down on the ice, Simmonds tried to jump over him, and his knee caught Giroux in the back of the head. They were facing in the same direction, but I looked at the video over and over again and the collision didn't seem severe enough to cause a lot of damage. I think Giroux might have been nailed by an earlier hit that didn't cause any problems right away.

Whenever you're dealing with a head injury, you've got a serious problem. Nowadays, they are a lot more cautious, a lot more conservative. There are tests a player has to pass before he's cleared to go back out there.

Protection might play a part in all this. Today all the players wear helmets and almost everybody is wearing a shield. Back in the day, when guys played without helmets, there was an understanding that you had to be careful about hitting another guy in the head. Guys looked each other in the eye and had a silent agreement: I will be careful with you and I expect you to be careful with me. Today, with everyone wearing a helmet, that understanding has gone away. That leads to less respect for the game and less respect for one another. Players today are more tempted to give a guy a shot to the head.

I also can't help wondering about the design of the helmet. Is it too snug? Are there openings for the impact to radiate out? Or is the helmet too tight, too solid, and keeping the impact confined? They might want to take a look at the shoulder pads guys are wearing now, too. Are they too big, too hard, considering the speed of the game and the impact of the collisions that are bound to happen? It's a serious problem. You can have $100 million in the bank, but what good is it if you spend the rest of your life in a daze because of repeated concussions?

Take Sidney Crosby. Before he got hurt, he was the best player in the league, but then he missed a whole season because of a concussion. You can't keep losing your best players to concussions and expect to draw big crowds.

There is one other thing they could do to cut back on those high-speed collisions, and that is widen the rink. That would give the skill players more room to skate and minimize the number of hits. They could widen the rink to 95 or maybe 100 feet. The problem here is that the owners might be reluctant to do that, because it would mean removing two rows of the best, most expensive seats in the arena.

The chances of doing that are slim and none, and slim just left town.

"BERNIE PARENT ONLY 'MISSES' THE BOAT"

It was déjà vu all over again. Bernie Parent pitched a shutout and the Flyers won their second Stanley Cup. How did the second one stack up with the first one? Bernie insisted that it was twice as good the second time around. (Originally published in the Philadelphia Daily News, *May 28, 1975)*

BUFFALO—Were the fish biting off Barnegat Light? Are they nibbling? Does the five-day forecast include small craft warnings? Is there enough beer in the cooler?

"You've gotta relax," Bernie Parent explained last night over the bedlam of another Stanley Cup championship. "You can't go out there tight. So I think about other things. Mostly, I think about my boat."

His boat. His ever-loving 45-foot boat. Beer in the cooler and bait in the buckets and gas in the tanks.

Gerry Desjardins, the other goalie, was so seasick he couldn't see straight. So Buffalo went with Roger Crozier, whose nerves have been known to twang like too-taut guitar strings.

And Parent? Parent ate a steak, took a nap, drank a cup of coffee, and went out and rode the roller coaster that is a Stanley Cup game.

He stopped 32 shots, which is how many Buffalo took. He stopped them with his glove, his stick, his chest, his arms, his skates. He stopped them from up close and from far away. He stopped the ones that came hurtling toward him straight on, and he stopped the ones that ricocheted off sticks and skates and darted in new directions.

"You ever see him play bad when it's a big game?" Bobby Clarke was asking people in the madhouse that was the Flyers' clubhouse afterward.

"It was just like last year, the last game against Boston. We could have played all night, and I don't think they could have scored."

It was a lot like last year, against Boston, when the Flyers snatched their first Stanley Cup with a sixth-game shutout.

"This time," Parent said, between television charades, "I enjoyed it more. Last year, we were in the clouds. This year we played the system."

Enjoyed it more? Desjardins was telling people before the sixth game he was beginning to hate the sport. Crozier was too grumpy to even express his feelings. Somehow it is beyond imagination's gloomiest reach to visualize Parent saying he "hated" the game.

"Bernie loves life too much to say that," Terry Crisp said, clutching a bottle of champagne by the throat. "The day he hates it, he'll quit."

Hate it? It is possible that Parent's love for the game explains his fantastic success, capped last night by the Conn Smythe Trophy that goes to the most valuable player in the championship series.

He takes the game seriously and himself lightly. A "big game player?" "Hey," he said, slumping into a corner of his locker. "Does that mean if you face 30 shots, instead of stopping 27, you have to stop 30?"

Parent was coming down now, out of the clouds, out of the giddy joyride that is the roller coaster. Making small jokes, because that is his nature.

"Fun?" he pondered the word carefully. "Sure, it's fun when you play for this team. You only face 26 or 27 shots a game, that's fun."

That's his equation for measuring fun. Play for a team that scraps and hustles and bumps and thumps and keeps the other team at a distance and it can be fun. Even if the other team sometimes gets 32 shots.

"Yeah," he said, "but we kept them from good angles. You don't win with one guy. During the season I only faced 26 or 27 shots a game. That's a team effort.

"The Smythe trophy has to go to somebody. But this is a team game. They say it's not the same, the second time around. They're wrong. It's twice as good.

"This is what the whole game is about."

And last night, unexpectedly, the end of May, the wearying skate-dragging end of May, and both teams unfurled a brilliant effort, etching it on fog-free ice.

The Sabres swarmed around Parent, testing him. They resembled hornets trying to sting some knight through his armor. He turned away 13 shots in the first period, and 13 more in the second, withstanding power play after power play.

And in the end, his teammates had trouble sorting out the best of what they had seen.

"He was beautiful," Clarke said, fidgeting with a cigarette. "He must have had 15 great saves."

"He plays good every game," said Ed Van Impe, blood thickening in a cut on the bridge of his nose. "Good every game and great some games. Tonight, he was great."

Parent talks about anticipation. He has trouble articulating just what it is he does. Van Gogh had the same trouble explaining his paintings.

But he will not let his nerves turn his arms and legs to stone, and that might be his greatest asset. "You're tight," he said, "and you make mistakes.

"If you're tight, you can't make the moves. Hey, you get ready and then you go out there and it's just like Doris Day sings, 'Que sera, sera.'"

Sure, Bernie, sure. But there must be some days when that afternoon nap is elusive as some nagging bumblebee, buzzing through the room. Some days when dreams come fitfully, full of shots that emerge from dark closets. Or does he make every save in the afternoon dreams?

"I don't dream about stopping shots," Parent said, smiling under that sweat-soaked mustache. "What do you want me to do…get tired before the game?"

The dreams can wait. Besides, they have trouble matching the reality of another Stanley Cup championship. "Geez," Parent said over and over, "This is what the game is all about."

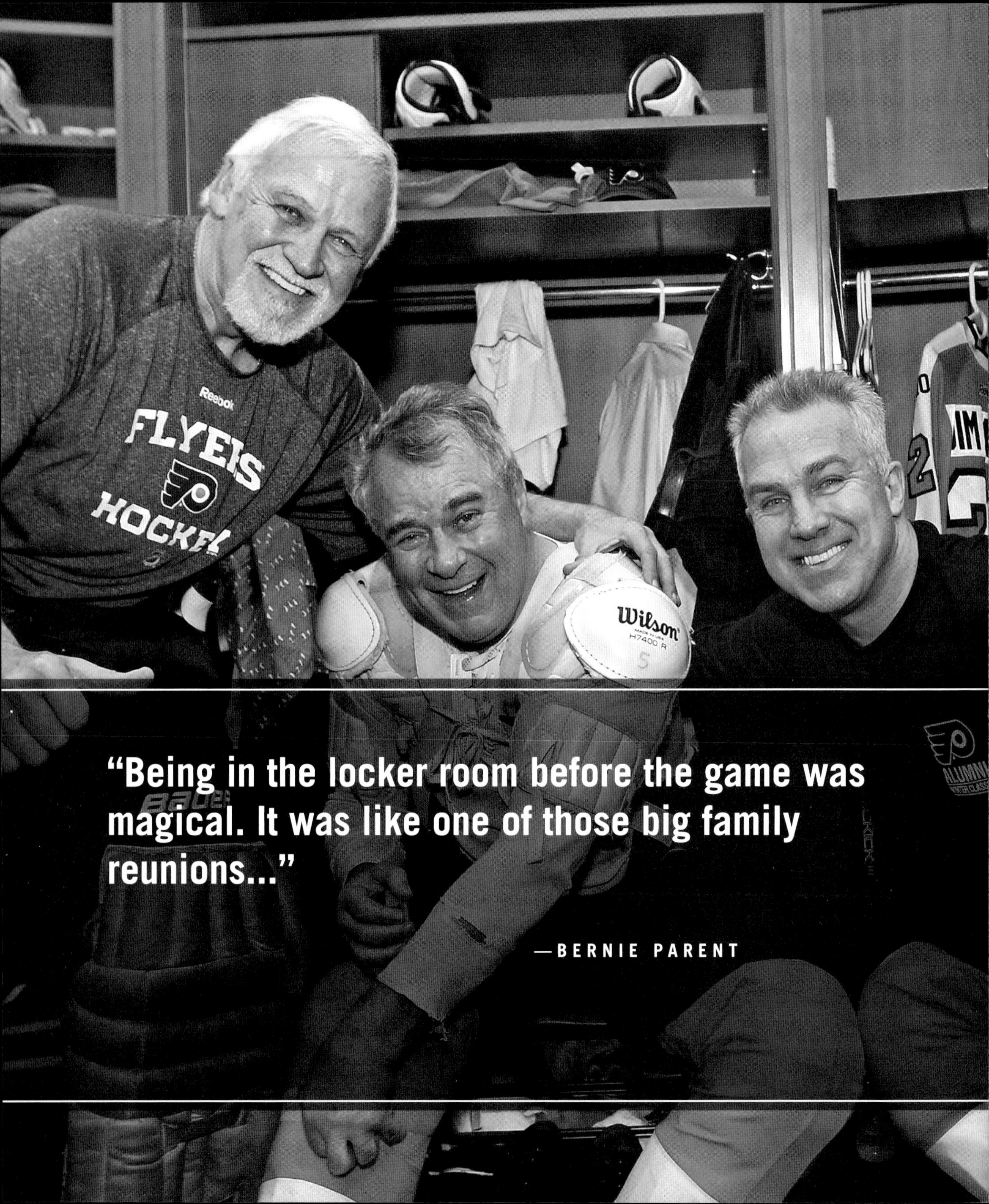

"Being in the locker room before the game was magical. It was like one of those big family reunions..."

—BERNIE PARENT

ALUMNI FUN, EH?

The moment I walked out of the Phillies dugout and headed for the rink they'd built near second base, I knew I had made the right decision. Citizens Bank Park was filled, and 45,000 fans were chanting my name.

It's like being in a hurricane. At first, the sound is in the distance, and then it comes closer and closer, louder and louder, until it wraps around you. "Bernie, Bernie, Bernie," they chanted. You cannot buy that feeling with all the money in the world.

It was New Year's Eve, and the alumni game was part of the Winter Classic, outdoors, in a baseball stadium converted into a hockey arena…and I almost missed it.

When they first asked me to play, I said no. I was thinking in terms of having to play a whole game. I was 66, for goodness sake, and I hadn't been in the nets except for the Flyers Wives Carnival. There I was facing three-year-old kids who were putting the puck past me and raising money for charity.

I would have 10 days to get ready. Ten days! After 30 years of not having the pads on? My pride was getting in the way. I was afraid of looking bad.

But then the e-mails started pouring in. They had announced some of the old-timers who would be playing in the game, and the fans wanted to know if I was going to play. I got hundreds and hundreds of e-mails.

Most of the people just wanted to see me back on the ice, one last time. I thought about it and figured if I played 10 minutes, how many shots would I have to face? Not many. And then I realized it wasn't my performance and my ego I ought to be thinking about—this was a chance to go back in front of the fans who had supported us through the years. Plus, the last time I played outdoors I was 12 years old, so that would be cool.

I talked it over with my advisor, Dean Smith, a truly good guy I trust. He felt strongly that I should play, even if it was just for 10 minutes. So I agreed to play. Then came the wait for my equipment to arrive. Some of it was in the Hall of Fame in Toronto, and some of it was in the Flyers' archives. Also, someone had to create and paint a white fiberglass mask with the Flyers logo on the side for me to wear.

When I walked out of that dugout, I had the mask propped back on my head. I didn't want to miss seeing or hearing anything.

I never did that when I played. I always kept the mask in place, mostly because I didn't want people to see any fear in my face. I didn't want the opponent to see some nervous tic of mine, the kind of thing poker players look for.

I wore my old brown pads and my old blocker. I wore the Winter Classic jersey, No. 1, just like old times. We practiced at the Skate Zone in Voorhees, New Jersey, and I worked my way up to 30 minutes, but that was about all I could handle.

The day before the game, they moved the starting time back two hours. We were going through what passed for a heat wave for the end of December. The afternoons were warm, around 55 degrees, and the ice was turning soft and slushy. So they moved the game from 1:00 PM to 3:00 PM, and then we caught a break when a lot of clouds moved in, hiding the sun. The temperature dropped around 10 degrees, and the ice held up.

Me, I'd have been happy playing on soft ice because it would slow the players down. We had a handful of guys in their sixties, and the Rangers had guys in their forties.

Was I worried about facing breakaways? Nah, the only time I was worried was when

Joe Watson was on the ice, playing defense. I'm kidding, but we always needled Joe. He turned out to be the oldest guy in the game at age 68. He was also the loudest, because when he yelled it would rattle windows in Camden, which is across the river.

Being in the locker room before the game was magical.

It was like one of those big family reunions, with all the different generations represented. The Flyers did such a great job in that sense. From the 1970s we had Clarke and Reggie Leach and Bill Barber. We had Orest Kindrachuk, who went out there wearing a shaggy black wig and a fake mustache to remind people of how he used to look. We had the Hound, Bob Kelly. We had guys like Don Saleski and Dave Schultz, not in uniform, but acting as ambassadors for the team.

From the 1980s we had Brian Propp and Rick Tocchet. From the 1990s we had guys like John LeClair and Mark Recchi, who once scored 123 points for the Flyers in one season.

Eric Lindros played, and that was special. When he came to the Flyers, the fans expected him to be Superman. He was a great player and then got sidetracked by injuries. His career got cut short by concussions.

He and Clarke didn't always get along, and people were on edge, wondering if any sparks would fly this time around. But Clarke handled it beautifully, even doing an interview with Lindros on the ice. Clarke even said that Eric belongs in the Hall of Fame.

Mark Howe was in there, too. He played 10 seasons for the Flyers and had just been inducted into the Hall of Fame, an honor that was well earned.

I found myself looking around and being overwhelmed. There were guys in their thirties, guys in their forties, guys in their fifties, and a fistful of guys in their sixties, and we all belonged to the same family, the Flyers family.

We joked around, telling pretty much the same old jokes because they never get stale. And then it was time to play the game. Lauren Hart had already done that wonderful duet with the image of Kate Smith on the big scoreboard, and the crowd was pumped.

WHEN I WALKED OUT OF THAT DUGOUT, I HAD THE MASK PROPPED BACK ON MY HEAD. I DIDN'T WANT TO MISS SEEING OR HEARING ANYTHING.

—BERNIE PARENT

"SCHULTZ: SHRINK WOULDN'T BELIEVE HIM ON THE RINK"

Dave Schultz, the Hammer, played the role of enforcer enthusiastically. Or so it seemed. He tried to explain how it felt to beat people up. (Originally published in the Philadelphia Daily News, *May 7, 1974)*

Dave Schultz assembles model airplanes in his spare time. Delicate, painstaking work. A guy has the patience, the dexterity, the hands to put together model airplanes… how come he uses those same hands to punch people in the head at the drop of a hockey puck?

"I've just got something in me," Schultz said yesterday, after the Flyers zipped through a workout at the Penn rink. "I have to psyche myself up. I'm not naturally like that.

"Sometimes being known for that makes me mad. And yet as far as winning hockey games, I'm glad I have it.

"I went home Sunday night and I lay there in bed, and I started thinking about Dale Rolfe. I felt sorry for him. Here's a guy who doesn't fight…a good, honest hockey player.

"And there, in front of all those people, and in front of a national television audience, he got the hell beat out of him. He must have felt awful.

"Something just changes me on the ice. It's not easy for me. Not like it's easy for a guy like Steve Durbano. A guy who fights in the street, a guy who likes to scrap. It's easier for a guy like that."

Bernie Parent's brother, the psychiatrist, would have his couch full with Schultz. "Ah yes, Mister Schultz, you seem like such a nice, well-mannered young man…I notice you took your skates off before getting up on the couch.

"Tell me, Mister Schultz, what happens to you when you slip into that uniform with the short, black pants? Does it remind you of something that happened in your childhood, something terrible, something that makes you lash out with your fists?"

The guilt feelings afterward would intrigue a prattle of psychiatrists. They intrigue guys like Larry Merchant, who used to commit his Freudian slips in this space and who now does his probing for the *New York Post*.

Do not invite Dave Schultz and Larry Merchant to the same city. Larry has decided that Schultz is some sort of Pavlovian dog gone mad, who froths at the mouth and savages people when the bell rings. Larry implies that Fred Shero whispers "Fetch" to Schultz and Dave scampers onto the ice to bring back an enemy player between his teeth.

It is a description that is going to rattle Schultz, who resented a "wrestling bear" analogy used to describe that wretched third game in New York. The next day Schultz made a figure 8 in the air four inches from a writer's face with the business end of his stick. At least it looked like a figure 8 between blinks.

Afterward, with the uniform off, Schultz discussed the issue calmly, as he did yesterday, when he was asked to explain how he had vanished in the sixth game of the brutal series.

"It's psychological," he said. "I'm not too fast, and I have not got that much talent. I get the puck and all of a sudden some guy is on me, time after time. Pretty soon, I'm saying, 'I can't even move' and I slow down more.

"The thing is, if a guy keeps pushing the whole way, he's gonna score. That night I never even tried to carry the puck. And I didn't get involved in a fight, because I knew I'd end up with more penalty minutes than the other guy for instigating it.

"I felt like I'd let the team down in New York. I came out Sunday, and I wasn't gonna go looking for something. But if it happened, I thought it would be against Butler. Or maybe Ron Harris.

"I figured I might as well try to kick hell out of Harris. He's supposed to be their tough guy. Not that he really is, but Emile Francis puts that pressure on him, saying he's the guy. And that's why I was happy he got a couple of goals to show he can do something else."

Schultz can do something else besides beat up people. Just ask the guys who play with him. Orest Kindrachuk and Don Saleski. They spent most of Sunday afternoon encamped in the New York zone.

"Everybody looks at Dave as a fighter," Saleski said, "but he scored 20 goals. He's got a good shot, he's not afraid to carry the puck. Dave Schultz, fighter, is a bad mark, but a good image in a way."

Schultz's reputation is like a cushion to the compact Kindrachuk, who was the closest eyewitness to the demolition job on Rolfe. "The big lummox," Kindrachuk said of Rolfe. "He wouldn't go down. He went down once and got back up. Most guys would have stayed down.

"The thing about Dave, he's got a real good wrist shot. Maybe the best wrist shot on the team. I always tell him to shoot, shoot, shoot."

Schultz doesn't shoot, shoot, shoot. He doesn't even shoot, shoot. But the "Action Line" of Kindrachuk, Schultz, and Saleski has scored five goals and racked up seven assists against Boston this year.

That's the sort of thing that punctures those theories about Shero keeping the snorting bull around to inspire other members of the herd who might be Ferdinand and prefer to smell the flowers. But that still leaves unexplained what happens to mild-mannered Dave Schultz once the game begins.

"He's such a quiet guy," Kindrachuk said. "Until he pulls on that sweater…and then he's a different man."

Maybe he's allergic to the wool? Or maybe it's psychological? Whatever, the Flyers want to keep him away from Bernie's brother, the psychiatrist, until after the Stanley Cup runneth over.

APPY NEW YEAR

There were flames and fireworks and each player had a banner with his name on it. The game started and pretty soon, here came Nick Fotiu of the Rangers, skating across the blue line and down the left side of the ice. Bam, he put this shot on net.

I reached out with my glove, stabbed at it, and knocked it away. The crowd went nuts, but the puck was just laying there, to my left, maybe three feet in front of me.

So I dove and smothered it. I landed on my left shoulder, which I had surgery on that June. I don't remember the doctors saying anything about diving on ice to cover a rebound, but it wouldn't have mattered. Instincts are instincts.

The crowd was chanting "Bernie, Bernie, Bernie," and the scoreboard showed a replay as the guys on the bench rapped their sticks against the boards to let me know they appreciated the effort.

I could feel my heart pounding inside my chest. My biggest fear was over. I had been haunted by the thought that the Rangers might score on the first shot they took, that the red light would go on, that the fans would groan in sympathy to this old man in the nets.

It wasn't long before Ron Duguay came in on another breakaway. Where was my defense, for goodness sake? You could hear the crowd moan, because the fans never liked Duguay when he played. He still had most of the long, flowing hair that he had back in the day.

He got to within 15 feet and then let the shot go. He could have picked a corner. Not the five hole, because he knew I wouldn't flop and there would be no space between my skates.

I was thinking, Lord, save me one more time. _And he did._

Duguay, bless his heart, shot it straight on and I stopped it with my stick as the crowd cheered.

The cheers were for me, as well as for Duguay, who showed a lot of class. The whole Rangers team showed class when you consider how bitter the rivalry was, how we'd played them 10 times in the playoffs, with the first time being that bloody 1974 semifinal series.

I made a kick save on a shot by Mark Messier, and I stopped a few others. By then I was panting, and it was time to call it a day. I lifted my mask, waved at the fans in the upper deck, skated in a small circle, and headed for the bench.

They were letting the clock run throughout the game, which was a good thing. They said I played 5:32 but it seemed a lot longer, definitely longer than the half hour in practice.

Mark LaForest replaced me in the nets, and he was great. He played one year for the Flyers when I was the goalie coach. He was little but quick, and he was also a good listener. We called him "Trees." See, not all hockey nicknames are dumb! LaForest stoned Nick Kypreos on one penalty shot. And Stan Blackburn, who played with two blockers because nerve damage that ended his career affected his glove hand, stopped Shjon Podein on a penalty shot.

About four minutes later, Lindros and LeClair charged down the ice on a 2-on-1. At the last second, with goalie John Vanbiesbrouck glued to the left post, Lindros passed the puck to LeClair, who tapped it into the open net.

The older fans remembered the Legion of Doom line, and they cheered the terrific play and were happy for Lindros, because now his homecoming was a joyful one. Eric looked like he could still play in the National Hockey League, big and fast, and strong on the puck. I think fans remembered that for his first three years with the Flyers, Eric was the best hockey player in the world. That was before he got hurt. So the reception he got was well deserved.

I changed into street clothes between periods and came back out later to rejoin my teammates on the heated bench. The game moved along quickly. Instead of putting a player in the penalty box when he did something wrong, they gave the other player a penalty shot.

Reebok
SiriusXm
ticketmaster
BRIDGESTONE

22
PARENT
1
SHER-WOOD

HOWE
2
EMIUM MEAT
SHER-WOOD

YOU'RE NEVER TOO OLD
TO GO AFTER YOUR PASSION. YOU HAVE
TO PREPARE. WILL YOU PERFORM THE
SAME WAY YOU DID 30 YEARS AGO?
OF COURSE NOT. BUT DON'T QUIT.

—BERNIE PARENT

CCM
10
BUNDY
BAUER
SHER-WOOD

After Neil Little had replaced LaForest in goal, the Rangers scored on a Glenn Anderson goal to cut our lead to 2–1. We made it 3–1 in the third period. What was really nice was the little kids who played a game on a small rink pounded their sticks on their boards when we walked off the ice between periods.

When it was over, Al Morganti, who has never been accused of being sentimental, picked the three stars of the game. He named me first, then Lindros, then LaForest, who stopped 16 shots.

It was the cherry on the sundae for me. Afterward, in the locker room, I told Joe Watson that I was getting a car for being star of the game and I was giving it to him. "Yeah," Joe shouted, "it's a toy car, this time."

You could tell Clarke wasn't happy because the Clarke-Barber-Leach line hadn't gotten a shot on goal. He said it was no fun when you can't play well anymore. But he was happy with the crowd and happy with the win.

When the television guys and the writers came around, I made sure to deliver a lesson. I told them that I was 66, that my career had ended suddenly thanks to an eye injury, and that I had fear coming out there that day. I conquered the fear, and that was the lesson: don't ever quit, don't ever give up.

You're never too old to go after your passion.

You have to prepare. Will you perform the same way you did 30 years ago? Of course not. But don't quit. What you believe, you can achieve. Too many people think they're too old to do something, so they don't bother trying. You've got to take some risks in life.

I told them about the magic that was in the room before the game, about the players being one big family. I told them I didn't want the red light to come on, that I had written a book about risk and fear, and that now, I'd had a chance to practice what I preached.

I did not tell them that I felt the same way I did 35 years ago in the hours before the game started. There were 45,000 people and that was terrific, but probably half the people were under 30, so they had never seen me play. All they knew about Bernie Parent was the retired number hanging from the rafters, the two

Stanley Cups, and the Broad Street Bullies reputation. But they had never seen me play with their own eyes, and if I let in two or three soft goals, what would they think of me? That I was a myth, that I was overrated. And what about the other half of the crowd, the fans who *had* seen me play? Wouldn't they expect me to look good in goal, to stop a breakaway?

That feeling of pressure never goes away. This time it was 45,000 people I did not want to disappoint. It's strange, because I heard the chants on my way to the rink, but once the game started, I didn't hear the crowd at all. I was too focused on what was happening on the ice.

I was proud of myself, because not once did I say, "Some fun, eh?" Sure, it wasn't a regular game, and it didn't count in the standings. But it was a game and I wanted to win it. And that is the bottom line.

"THE SHOOTER COMES OF AGE"

The Flyers made a few changes after winning their first Stanley Cup. The best move was bringing in Reggie Leach, who scored 61 goals. Leach hid his feelings deep inside him. He sat still for a rare interview about growing up in Riverton. (Originally published in the Philadelphia Daily News, *May 6, 1976)*

They are going to stage a "day" for Reggie Leach in Riverton, Manitoba, this summer. Sweep the cobwebs off the chairs at the Sandy Bar Hotel. Sweep the cobwebs off some of the customers, too.

"It's the kind of place," Leach said yesterday, "where you can go into a pub right now and see the same people every morning when it opens…and go back at 11:00 at night and the same people will be in the same chairs. That's the way life is there."

It is a bleak life. The men shuttle freight north all winter, sit around the pub all summer. Tempers fray, fists fly.

"A tough place to grow up," Leach said. "The best thing that ever happened to me was leaving Riverton. Otherwise, I might still be one of the local yokels sitting around the bar."

As bleak as it was, as grim as it was, Leach is happy to be going home for the celebration. Even if the parade is three cars and a pickup truck, even if the confetti comes from the lone Yellow Page in the telephone directory. Leach's habits, Leach's attitudes, were chiseled out of the bleak granite of Riverton and he is ill at ease in big cities, in big crowds.

"I don't like to be bugged," he said yesterday. He scored 61 goals this season. He has scored a goal in eight consecutive playoff games. In New York, they would be building a statue on Broadway. He'd own two nightclubs, a disco, an ice cream parlor, four racehorses.

In Philadelphia he shuns the limelight, although he did do commercials for a morning newspaper. Ironically, he handled the dialogue all right. The tough part was slapping the puck into the net when the strobe lights went on.

That is ironic, because Leach looks like he could put the puck in the net blindfolded, swinging a Sunday *Inquirer*, wearing snowshoes.

"I've got a lot of confidence now," he said. "All I need is one good shot and I'll put it in. Like Tuesday, the only good shot I had all night, I put it in. Clarke gave me the puck and I fired. Kept it on the ice.

"You have that feeling, you come to the rink early, you get ready for the game, you feel good in the warmups, you're more sure with the puck, you're not fighting it at all."

There is a temptation to demean what Leach has achieved because he has Bobby Clarke poking the puck loose for him. But if Clarke furnishes the bullets, Leach must still aim and pull the trigger.

"I can release the puck as fast as anyone, I guess," Leach said. "My biggest thing, I suppose, is that within 15 or 20 feet of the net, I'm deadly."

He did not teethe on a hockey stick. He did not crawl, then walk, then shoot his rattle 120 miles an hour. He worked at it and worked at it, which will come as a surprise to people who think Leach is just a bland little gunner.

"He spent hours and hours shooting the puck," Clarke said. "He was always a great skater. But he'd work on shooting. Hang pails from the corners of the net and shoot at them."

"I had a shed where I lived," Leach recalled. "I'd make ice and shoot the puck three hours a day. Make targets. Have some guys over and have shooting contests.

"I played the game. I was good when I was 12, 13. Played with guys 14. But I never thought I'd be a pro until I got to Flin Flon and played with Clarke.

“I was scouted by Detroit. They sent me to Wayburn when I was 15. Quit school. School was bad for me. I was a disturber, anyway. In Junior B, I quit at Christmas time. Homesick.

“But the next year they sent me to Flin Flon. I had good years, mainly because of Clarke. The coach said, ‘Stick with it, you’ll amount to something.’

“When I played in junior, I could shoot from the blue line and score. I think I had a better shot in junior than I have now. I was a little crazy in junior, though, a cocky little bugger. You name it, I did it.”

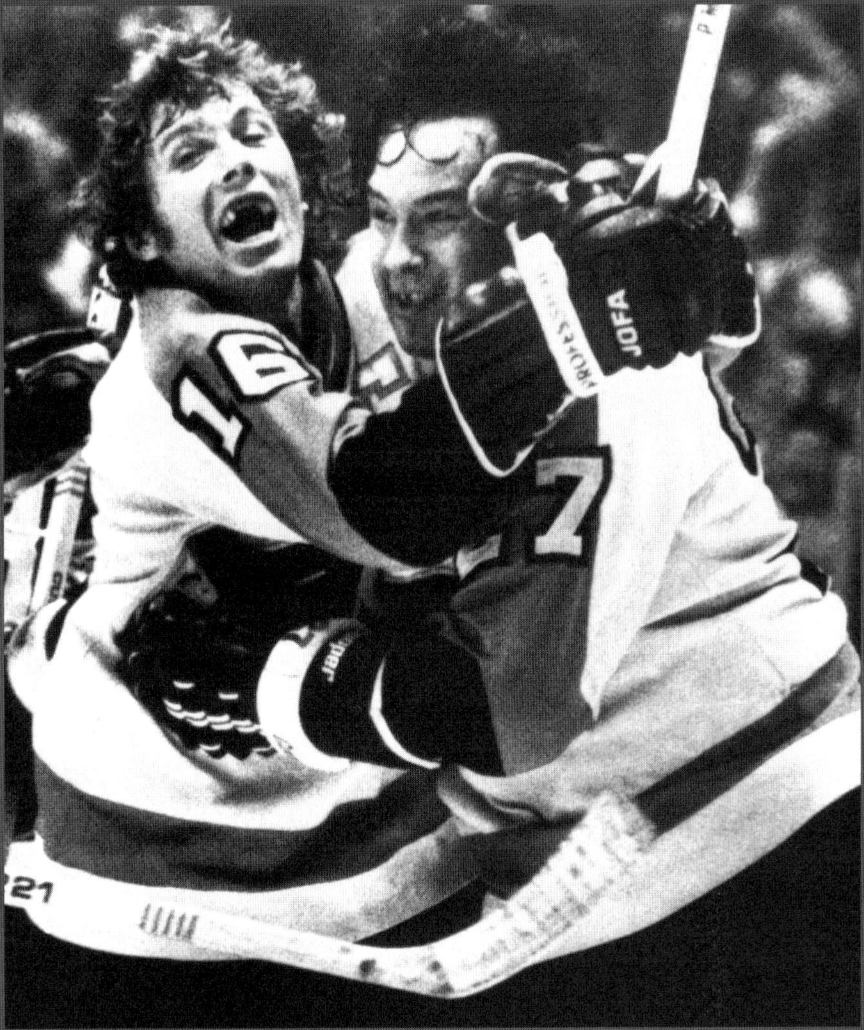

One summer, Clarke had to bail him out of a jam. “Got home on Friday,” Leach said. “By Saturday I was in trouble. I was 16. A bunch of us were at this Chinese place, drinking. A guy said something to my buddy. I got involved.

“He came at me with a ketchup bottle. I took his plate and dumped it on his head. That’s how it started. On Monday, I had to go to court. They would have locked me up, but I called Clarke in Flin Flon and he wired the money and got me out.”

Clarke bailed Leach out then. He would do it one more time, bailing him out of the prison that was the California Golden Seals, encouraging the Flyers to trade for him. And Clarke argues vehemently with critics who belittle Leach as a one-way player.

“With his ability,” Clarke said, “if they want him to be a defensive player, he could do it. He’s big, he’s strong. But what’s the good if a guy is capable of scoring 60, only scoring 20? I don’t expect him to score 60 every year, but he can still be an important player.”

The hours of shooting the puck against the shed prepared him for his role as a scorer. There were few distractions in those days.

“Ahhhh, you grow up in a big city, you might get stuck on some corner,” Leach said. “Look around the league, a lot of guys come out of a lot of little towns…where there was nothing else to do but play hockey and that’s it.”

Next year and the harsh expectations can wait. There’s a championship to scuffle for and then, that “day” in Riverton, Manitoba. Who says you can’t go home again?

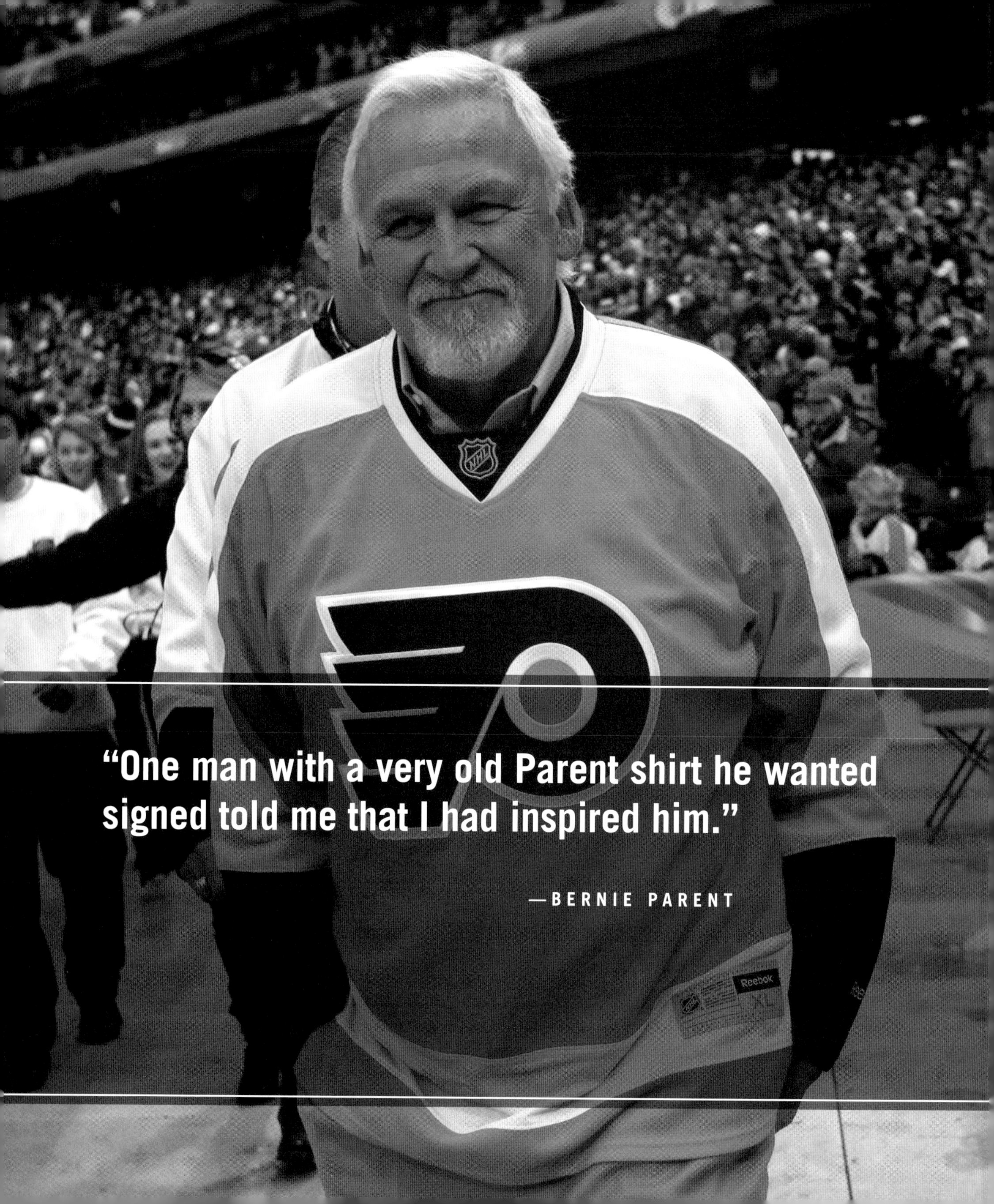

“One man with a very old Parent shirt he wanted signed told me that I had inspired him.”

—BERNIE PARENT

CHAPTER TEN

LIFE IS GOOD

My career ended suddenly with the blade of a hockey stick jabbing into my right eye, slashing the tendons, and destroying the lens.

I had been drinking too much, and now I plunged into depression. Would professional therapy have helped me? Should I have looked for a psychiatrist to help me solve my problems and yank me out of the darkness?

No. I never believed in a shrink and never will. I've shared the story about how Freddie Shero thought it might help the Flyers and how I chased the guy out before he took one step into our locker room.

Part of that was the time and place. We were the Broad Street Bullies; we spread fear into the hearts and minds of the teams we played. We didn't change when we went on the road the way some teams do.

After most games there was blood on the ice. Most of the time it was the other guys' blood, some of the time it was our own. We had nicknames like Hammer and Hound and Moose and we were tough. How would it have looked if somehow it came out that we had a shrink working with us? It would have chipped away at our mystique. It would have destroyed our image. In those days, having a team psychologist would have been seen as a weakness.

Personally, I needed help. But I could never see myself sitting down with a stranger, one-on-one, to share my problems, to look for help. I'd like to think I can review things in my own mind, figure out solutions, and march forward. The truth is, finding that self-help program made all the difference. It was a place I could share my thoughts, and where I could listen to other people talk about their struggles. It was a group dynamic.

As part of my work with the Flyers now, I occasionally visit people in the hospital with serious illnesses. It's a tough thing for me to do. Sometimes I feel like if someone has cancer and an athlete comes by and tries to make him feel better, it doesn't really work. But if someone comes in who has the same disease and shares his problems, then you have a chance to make some progress.

Sure, we had some players who were not playing up to their full potential from time to time. But I never thought some sports psychologist could come in and solve our problems. That was up to our teammates to do. We'd get out on the ice, in practice, and we talked it over—why are you not turning the right way? Why are you not thinking the right way in certain situations?

We'd practice techniques. We overcame problems that way. Take a guy like Rick MacLeish, who was such a talented skater who made things look easy. There were times when he wasn't going all out and we knew it.

That's when someone like Bobby Clarke would step in. He wouldn't point a finger at MacLeish. What he would do is say out loud how big the game was, how important the game was, and how we had to get going at both ends of the ice. Rick would get the message and respond, which is why his numbers were so impressive in the playoffs.

Going to Rexy's was our group therapy. It was so much easier to talk about the way guys were playing in a joint with sawdust on the floor than it was pointing out things at the rink. Nobody resented getting criticized if it happened at Rexy's.

Things are very different today. The players union is stronger, much more powerful than it's been in the past. It stood up to the owners when they wanted to change the divisions, which would have affected some old rivalries. The players didn't want the playoff format changed either, so the owners had to put that off for another year.

Back in the day, the coach had tremendous power. It was his way or the highway.

Nowadays, a coach has to know the game, but he also has to know how to motivate, how to deal with different personalities, who to pat on the back, and who to kick in the butt.

Before the Winter Classic in 2012, the outdoor game at Citizens Bank Park, HBO ran a series called *24/7* where they followed the Flyers and the Rangers for three weeks leading up to the game.

Most people who talked to me loved it. Some people hated it. The ones who loved it really enjoyed getting an inside look at what goes on in the locker room. The ones who hated it didn't like the language used by the coaches, Peter Laviolette and John Tortorella. Every fifth word began with the letter *F*.

As we would say back home, it was no effing good to hear all that. Freddie Shero never cursed. He got his point across quietly. Between periods he would say, without naming names, that we got beat on a goal because somebody was lazy getting back. The guys all knew who he was talking about.

Coaches are different, and they all have different styles. That doesn't mean one guy is right and the other wrong. I like Laviolette because he's doing a heckuva job. Am I going to judge him because of the language he uses in the room? No. I judge him by the results and how the players respond to him.

A coach like Shero was a master at dealing with different personalities. He was compassionate, and the players knew that. He was also very humble, which is why he would go and hide when we won the Cup, letting the spotlight shine on the players because that's where he felt it belonged.

If that HBO show was supposed to build interest in the sport, it didn't work. The television ratings were great in Philadelphia, but nationally they were the lowest in the history of the Winter Classic.

I think some of the stuff they showed had a negative effect. They showed some Russian kid on the Rangers who scored a goal and used his stick like a rifle to celebrate. Bam, he got penalized. Then they showed him apologizing to his teammates.

To me, that's negative. Why show this around the world? When you watch the news, all you see is negative stuff. I stopped watching the news about 15 years ago. There was so much garbage on. The media always looks for bad news. If the main thing they're showing is coaches dropping the f-bomb, that's negative. Why not show the beauty of the game? That other stuff, the cursing, that should stay behind closed doors.

I know they showed one of the hockey rinks that Mr. Snider rescued so that the kids in his youth hockey program had a place to practice and play, and that was good. The man had a vision about hockey in Philadelphia and it's amazing how the story has played out.

They told me that the Russian goalie, Ilya Bryzgalov, was the star of that HBO show.

He's a funny dude—at one point he talked about the universe being humongous, only he pronounced it *hue-mang-US*. But he's not a dumb guy. I've talked to him and I like him. He wrapped his arm around me at the Christmas party and he thanked me for my support. I always say good things about him. Look, he came here from Phoenix, and there's no comparison between the two cities as far as hockey is concerned. The pressure is greater here, and expectations are higher here.

He's big, he reads plays well, and he moves well. He's going to be fine. Will he hit some valleys along the way? Of course he will, but I have confidence he will always bounce back.

Mr. Snider gave him a $51 million contract. Then Lavlioette showed some courage by not starting him against the Rangers in the Winter Classic. That was a tough decision, but he just felt that Sergei Bobrovsky gave the team a better chance to win that game, so that's who he started.

I come to the home games. I greet the fans, I sign autographs. Then, Bob Kelly and I visit some of the suites during the first period. We walk in, pose for a picture, sign an autograph or two, and tell the people to enjoy the game. I enjoy meeting people, so I enjoy doing it.

After the alumni game that was part of the Winter Classic, people wanted to let me know how much they enjoyed it. We had 45,000 people there. Bobby Clarke said that wouldn't happen in any other city in North America, and he was right.

The next week, the Flyers had a Saturday afternoon game against Ottawa. Gary Dornhoefer and I signed autographs before the game. We do it near Section 124, standing in front of the shop that sells Flyers gear. There's an official photographer there, and he puts all the photos on the Internet where, if people like them, they can buy them.

At first, people just stepped up and asked us to sign their jersey or their ticket stub. Pretty soon, the supervisor of ushers, a good guy named Jim, organized a line that snaked down the corridor past some of the concession stands. That day, the photographer took 220 pictures.

A guy wearing a Chris Pronger shirt asked Dorny if he remembered a certain game against Boston, 30 years ago. Dorny told him he couldn't remember what he had for breakfast.

A minute later, though, he remembered the best round of golf he ever shot, a 63 on an easy course in Canada.

One man came up and spoke to me in French. He told me how proud he was when I dove for the puck in the alumni game. I told him I was more proud that I got up. I asked his wife if she spoke French, and she shrugged bashfully and shook her head, no. And then she said, "Je t'aime." And even my friend Stan Hochman knew that meant, "I love you."

Larry Zeidel came by with a friend. The friend was carrying the Stanley Cup ring Larry won playing for Detroit. It was a much simpler ring than they make now, mostly silver with hardly any diamonds. But you knew it meant the world to him because he made sure his friend held onto it tightly. "I was 40, Bernie was 21, and they roomed us together," Zeidel said. He didn't tell anybody how that worked out, which was okay with me.

Most of the young people were wearing Flyers jerseys. Someone counted 42 Claude Giroux jerseys, so he won the unofficial popularity contest. There were a handful of Chris Pronger shirts, some Danny Briere shirts (he had a Gordie Howe hat trick that game, three goals and a fight), and I even spotted a couple Bryzgalov and Bobrovsky shirts. There was one woman wearing a Nittymaki jersey. There were lots of Winter Classic shirts, as well as some throwback shirts: Eric Lindros, John LeClair, and others.

Every once in a while someone showed up wearing an IVB Bernie Parent Savers Club windbreaker, the orange jacket they gave away when somebody opened a $50 savings account back in the day. One guy got my autograph on a Parent shirt, and then said, "Some fun, eh?" That showed me he'd been around a while.

When people told me what they thought of the alumni game, the word I heard most was *awesome*. Dornhoefer told someone that I stood up in that game because I'd taken three Viagara before the puck dropped. That tells you Dorny's jokes have not improved over the years.

One man with a very old Parent shirt he wanted signed told me that I had inspired him.

He said he had not laced up a pair of skates in 30 years, but the day after the alumni game he went out skating. He said his legs were killing him after he was done, but it was the best thing he ever did.

And in the middle of the organized chaos, a man came by holding his little girl in his arms. She was sobbing. He ignored the line and came right up to me. "Bernie," he said, "can you do me a favor? Can you convince my little girl that those escalator steps are okay?"

The escalator that leads to the upper deck at Wells Fargo Center is long and steep. I could see how a little girl might be afraid of it. So I asked her, "Would you like me to go up with

A guy wearing a Chris Pronger shirt asked Dorny if he remembered a certain game against Boston, 30 years ago. Dorny told him he couldn't remember what he had for breakfast.

you?" And she stopped crying and nodded her head.

So I walked them to the escalator and then talked to her the whole way up, telling her how pretty she was and how much she was going to enjoy the game. Before she knew it, we were at the top and she was fine.

I went back downstairs, got back in place to sign more autographs, and somebody said, "One more save for Bernie."

An attractive woman told me I was getting better looking every year, which was a nice thing to hear. I weighed 195 during my playing days, and I weighed a little over 200 for the alumni game, so the equipment still fit. I don't like diets, because they ultimately end and then it's tough to maintain the weight loss. So I just cut out sugar and things made with white flour from my diet. And it worked. I go to the gym every so often, just to work out a little and maintain my cardiovascular health.

A man came up with his six-year-old son. I showed the little boy my ring and his eyes got wide. The father said, "That's a Stanley Cup ring. Maybe someday soon we'll see another one of those."

Bob Kelly joined us, wearing a slick dark suit. He has to get dressed up because he runs the "Mites on Ice" promotion between periods. At one point, Kelly grabbed a toy hockey stick from a kid and jabbed him in the ribs with it, just for old times' sake. The kid was puzzled, but his father got the joke.

It was getting close to game time, so Kelly assigned a couple of ushers to mark the end of the autograph line. They got bored and walked

BERNIE
PARENT
1
TOYOTA
FOX
29
NEWS

I SMOKED MY CIGAR AND DRANK MY DIET SODA AND WATCHED THE GAME ON A BIG-SCREEN TELEVISION SET. THE FLYERS WON IN OVERTIME. LIFE IS GOOD.

—BERNIE PARENT

away, so the line was still long as game time approached.

A couple came up with pictures from the alumni game for me to sign, and in one photo I'm walking to the rink over a blue tarp. I told the woman that the blue part was really water, and that day I felt like I could walk on water. She laughed.

Jim, the supervisor, finally assigned two trusty ushers to mark the end of the line. He looked proudly at us and said, "They'll be doing this when they're 100." I don't know about that, but I do know I enjoy meeting people. The photographer told someone, "Bernie never turns anyone away. It's one last autograph, one last photo, every time."

Jim led us to the executive offices and we sat down near the elevator to catch our breath. There were some more photos and pucks to autograph and we did that while a pretty girl from the community relations staff joined us. She had started her career as an intern but had worked her way up to a full-time job, and she was going to whisk us through the visits to the suites.

We headed up to the top level and then the sprint began. We got to the first suite as Lauren Hart was singing the two anthems. She is a terrific singer, probably the best one in hockey. Dornhoefer said, "She always brings her A game," and he's right. We stuck around for less than a minute, shook some hands, and then bingo, we were off to the next suite.

I told Dorny we let him go in first, just in case somebody's got a gun. In one suite they were celebrating a kid's birthday. In another they were celebrating a young man's college graduation.

Hustling down the corridors, waitresses would stop me, hug me, or pat me on the cheek. "I was crying," one waitress said, thinking about the alumni game. "Me, too," I told her.

In one suite a guy told me he was worried about Bryzgalov, because he was talking about missing his family in that HBO series. I told him not to worry, that Bryzgalov would be fine.

We visited 14 suites in 32 minutes, which is a pretty fast pace. We had to finish before the first period ended, and we made it with about 40 seconds to spare.

Then it was time to relax in the Wells Fargo Cigar Bar. They keep a table reserved for me and my friends. Tim, who looks after me and likes to say he's my bodyguard, was there along with his wife. He has a farm in South Jersey, and we were there the day before the alumni game. His son put on an old Three Stooges movie and it was like old times.

I lit up an Ashton Cabinet, a good cigar. Deena, one of my favorite people, brought me a diet soda. She's a terrific waitress and she hangs around our area making sure we're not bothered. Somebody handed me a Flyers cap to sign. I looked at it and saw it had Kelly's autograph on the bill. I told the guy that the Hound signed it, and that knocked down the value of it. He laughed.

Some guy asked me how I felt the day after the alumni game, and I said, "Well, I can usually romance four women after a game, but that day I had to stop at three."

Pretty soon, along came Bob Dailey, the guy we called "The Count." He was about 6'10" on skates. As soon as he sat down, he said, "Bernie, you looked like crap out there in the alumni game." Some things never change. I remember the days when we used to practice at the Class of '23 rink at the Penn campus. We practiced in the mornings when it was bitterly cold inside that building. I'd be stiff as a board and here came Dailey firing shots at me. I'd scream at him and tell him I wanted to hear those shots banging off the glass behind me, and he'd just laugh and keep shooting.

I smoked my cigar and drank my diet soda and watched the game on a big-screen television set. The Flyers won in overtime. Life is good.

Some guy asked me how I felt the day after the alumni game, and I said, "Well, I can usually romance four women after a game, but that day I had to stop at three."

"PARENT SAVES SOULS NOW WITH SELF-HELP BOOK"

Decades after the sudden end to his gaudy career, Bernie Parent decided to write a self-help book based on his own experiences and his struggle against drinking and depression. He is in demand as a motivational speaker and has been clean and sober for more than 30 years. (Originally published in the Philadelphia Daily News, *April 22, 2011)*

If you feel lost and gloomy, wandering in some thick, dark forest, trudging in circles, Bernie Parent wants to lead you out of that forest and into the sunshine. And no, he is not selling you a compass or a GPS app for your iPhone. Or maybe he is.

Yep, that Bernie Parent, the last Flyers goalie to lug the Stanley Cup around the ice in a victory lap. The guy who watched The Three Stooges on game days. The guy who began every sweaty postgame interview with a chuckling, "Some fun, eh?"

Parent has written a self-help book designed to steel you to overcome fear, take risks, unleash your inner wolf, and find fulfillment. It is called *Journey Through Risk and Fear*. He wrote it in collaboration with writer Michele Paiva and his manager, Dean Smith. Why three authors? Because the strength of the wolf is in the pack.

"A lot of people are struggling," Parent, 66, said the other day. "They're lost in the woods, going in circles. It seems like there's no way out. I look at my life and there's something there that could encourage people to come out of it.

"I lost an eye, my career ended suddenly, I hit bottom."

He looked for answers in the bottom of beer bottles and found nothing but headaches. He embraced a self-help group and has been clean and sober for 31 years.

"When my career ended," he said sadly, "all I knew how to do was play hockey. I had no business experience. I knew no one who could help me. Finally, I looked in the mirror and I saw a human being, not just a hockey player, and that was the turning point."

That, and reading a self-help book called *The Secret*, a gift from one of his kids.

"It changed my life," he said. "It took me back to when I was a little kid. My purpose in life was to win the Stanley Cup. And that never changed. I played in Niagara Falls. I played for the Bruins, for the Flyers, for Toronto, went into the World Hockey Association, and then back with the Flyers. And except for that time in the WHA, my purpose was to win the Stanley Cup.

"What you need is a purpose. You have to get rid of the fear, you have to be willing to take risks. Then, bingo, the magic happens. You meet people you didn't know existed. You surround yourself with people who have great ideas and reaching for their goals."

Most nights, Parent was a magician in pads, smooth, slick, cat-quick. He had 12 shutouts the season they won their first Stanley Cup. Had 12 more the next year, when they won it again. That's 12 more shutouts than the Flyers' goalies had this season.

The Flyers initially sent out rookie Sergei Bobrovsky against the Sabres for the playoffs, and have now turned to veteran Brian Boucher. "The best way to approach a game is to be prepared," Parent said. "Not being nervous, it's being excited. Once you're excited, good things start to happen."

Maybe Parent can send along some old Stooges films to help. "Let's face it," he chuckled, "those guys were funny. Still laugh when I watch 'em. I did my preparation the night before a game. Game day, I wanted to laugh, to carry that good feeling to the rink."

Parent spends most of his time on his boat, "The French Connection," when he's not out and about making appearances. If it's good to be the king, it's not bad to be the last Flyers goalie to win the Stanley Cup. Doors open, meal tabs vanish, babes flock. Is there some small part of him that wants to retain that distinction?

"Nooooo," he said swiftly. "There is nothing more I would love than to see the Flyers win the Cup and have a parade again. I think back to when we first came to town and rode down Broad Street on a float. Ten people watched, plus a Great Dane and a poodle. A few years later, there were 2 million people at the parade.

"Winning that first one, at home, that was awesome. The second one, we won in Buffalo. And then we flew home with the Cup sitting in the middle of the aisle. I sat there and looked at it, and looked at it, and it was beautiful."

ACKNOWLEDGMENTS

I would like to thank Dean Smith, Bernie Parent's friend and advisor, for all his help, from start to finish. I would like to thank the Flyers' crackerjack public relations staff headed by Zack Hill, especially Brian Smith and archivist Brian McBride. Bob Clarke's foreword was a highlight for me. The Winter Classic alumni game gave me a chance to reconnect with so many of the Broad Street Bullies, and it didn't hurt when Bernie blanked the Rangers and was voted star of the game. Finally, credit is due to Jack Chevalier's *The Broad Street Bullies* and Bill Fleishman's *Bernie!*

—Stan Hochman